The People's History
Around
Washington

by

Stuart Miller & George Nairn

The Village Blacksmiths
The village blacksmiths was a standard postcard feature. For many years it was in the hands of the Dobson family. In the 1950s it became a pottery and a cafe/restaurant. Evelyn Keen in her brief childhood recollection in *Bridging the Gap* (1988) says: 'Lunch time at school was spent watching the Smithy in the village shoeing horses. (I remember) the smell as he placed the hot shoes on the hoof, and the smoke rising from it and then the hissing as he then placed the shoe in the water to cool!' In this view the ghostly figure to the right has walked through time! The exposure length has blurred the image. On the other hand it might be the ghost of Jane Atkinson – the witch of Washington Village!

Previous page:
Walter Willson's Swans
Walter Willson's was in Station Road next to the Celtic Club. These swans visited the shop regularly from Barmston Willows pond. This time they have brought cygnets with them though. 'Smiling Service' it says above the door and windows.

Copyright © Stuart Miller & George Nairn 1998

First published in 1998 by

The People's History
Suite 1
Byron House
Seaham Grange Business Park
Seaham
Co. Durham
SR7 0PW

ISBN 1 902527 30 5

Contents

The Ferry Boat Inn
This is one of many inns and taverns along the river which catered originally for the keelmen and the pitmen. This is a back-yard view. There is a frontal view of the Ferry Boat Inn elsewhere in this book. This rear view gives a better idea as to the age of the building.

Acknowledgements

We both embarked upon this book for different reasons. One of the authors, George Nairn, has collected old postcards and photographs of north eastern places and scenes for many years and is fascinated by the regional heritage in all its guises. The other, Stuart Miller, is a professional historian who knew surprisingly little about Washington before working on this book, but got lost there so frequently as to have a developed a sort of expertise.

We must both acknowledge readily the help we have received from a number of people:

John Wood and the friendly staff of Washington Library for help and guidance regarding sources, and for making available a number of Library photographs for reproduction here and which are duly credited. Ashley Sutherland and John Wood for their careful proof-reading and helpful comments.

Joan Nichol for her memories of times past in Old Washington which brought to life the chapel community in particular.

The Beamish Photographic Archive for their generous assistance. John Woodall, Betty and Jack English and Nancy Godwin for their permission to reproduce various pictures and for their helpful advice. Dorothy Rand for her help with proof reading in the final stages. We would also like to thank the Forte Family and Miss Edith Forster.

We hope you enjoy this exploration of Washington.

Stuart Miller
George Nairn

Introduction

The purpose of this introduction is threefold. First of all to explain the origin and purpose of the book. Secondly to explain the structure and general background history of Washington itself, because that is complex to the outsider. Finally, since this is essentially a book of postcards and photographs it will be helpful to make some points about the value of such pictorial material to the historian and general reader.

Washington: Definition, Boundaries and Communities

According to the antiquarian and historian Fordyce the definition of Washington was as follows:

'The parish of Washington is part of the Harraton Sub-district of the Chester-le-Street Union, bounded by Jarrow on the north, by Monkwearmouth on the south-east, by Houghton on the south and by the chapelries of Birtley and Lamesley on the west.' (1857)

In fact our definition has been a good deal more rigorous and exclusive than that of Fordyce. We have devoted our attention to the 5,610 acre area covered by the old Washington Development Corporation. That area was bounded by the A1(M) to the west, the River Wear to the south east, Gateshead Urban District to the north and Houghton-le-Spring Urban District to the south. The main section excluded from Fordyce's area by this definition is Springwell – which is covered in another perfectly good book of photographs in its own right.

This modern area includes the historic settlements of North and South Biddick, Fatfield, Barmston, Cox Green, Washington Village, Washington Station and High and Low Usworth. These were settlements which may have been originally rural and agrarian (and still often bear the marks of that past) but had evolved on the basis of the riverine coal export trade, coal mining and other industries such as iron founding and chemicals.

There is little point here in trying to summarise the history of Washington because this book is presented in such a way as to provide the reader with a reasonably fluent coverage of the various aspects anyhow. What is particularly confusing about Washington though is that it really has three overlapping histories ie. as a group of ancient pre-industrial rural settlements, as industrialising modern communities and then as a planned and contrived New Town made up of a number of 'villages'. Some fragments of the rural past remain, the great industrial past of the area has been all but obliterated but the Washington New Town is very evident.

This means that, for example, there is considerable ambiguity about the names of the residential settlements. For its villages and industrial estates the Development Corporation adopted a range of names some of which were associated with names and places in the area but which do not match the traditional settlement boundaries and communities. Hence the appearance of imported names like Columbia, Albany and Concord, the elevation of existing local names like Ayton, Lambton and Sulgrave and the disappearance, technically speaking, of names like New Washington. So if you really want to understand the layout of Washington you should stop by the roadside and study one of those huge map boards which pretend to rescue the lost motorist from an eternal circuit of the area.

The story of the New Town is well told by Stephen Holley the General Manager of the Development Corporation in *Washington: Quicker by Quango* (1983). The area was designated a new town by the Ministry of Housing and

Local Government in 1964. The objective was to counteract the impact of the ailing industries, high unemployment, dereliction and environmental pollution. The Development Corporation was established in the same year and lasted until 1987 when its functions were taken over by the Borough of Sunderland. Washington became part of the Sunderland Metropolitan District in 1974. The plan was to integrate the scattered communities of the area into a planned urban environment based on an axial network of primary and secondary roads with an eventual population of up to 80,000. There were to be 18 distinct residential areas accommodating about 4500 people each, and ten industrial estates. The hub of all of this was to be the Galleries, a complex of shops and offices.

The purpose of this book is to revive memories of the older Washington in the days before the Development Corporation. However the pace of change in the area has been so great and the effects so considerable that we have felt it necessary to extend our coverage into the 1960s.

Images of the Past: Postcards and Photographs as Evidence

The essence of the book is a series of pictures many of which are from postcards. There are very many private and official photographs though as well. This requires a comment or two about the value of such material to the historian.

The first picture postcards appeared from the 1st September 1894 but the great age of the picture postcard began in 1902 when the requirement that the whole of one side must bear both the stamp and the addressee's name and address was removed. The floodgates were opened to the new divided back, picture postcard. The volume of postcards sent and the nature of their pictorial subjects is quite amazing to modern eyes. There were essentially three types of postcards. There were nationally mass produced cards of subjects such as the Town Hall, municipal park, harbour entrance and so on. Local photographers would produce pictures of schools, brass bands, football teams and local streets which would be sold by local shopkeepers. Finally private individuals would also commission professional photographers to produce cards of their families or some other personal subject and then they would send them to friends and relations. There are examples of all of these in this book. Cards were used in the way that 'phone calls are used today. In the Edwardian period there could be up to ten postal deliveries a day in some areas as well so the scope for postcards was much enhanced.

Most of the postcards represented in this book are topographicals – as opposed to commemoratives, personal or humorous cards. That is to say they are general views of riverside scenes, urban streets, collieries and their surroundings, significant buildings and so forth. Present day views as to the suitability of subjects for postcard sales differ from those of the past. Some of the most mundane street scenes are represented here. From a historian's point of view though that is what makes them of interest. Postcards of disasters are quite common. In the Washington area there were mining accidents and disasters enough. One of these, the Glebe Colliery explosion and fire of 1908, is well represented here (with a bulk purchase discount offer as well!). Official postcards were produced for some purposes and this collection includes one such from a 'squaddie' at Usworth Camp.

Wherever possible we have selected card views with people and activity displayed. In a number of cases it is obvious that that was just what the photographers were trying to avoid. Of course the range of postcards available depended partly upon the selection of saleable scenes by speculative photographers such as R. Johnston and Son and Messrs. Auty and Hastings

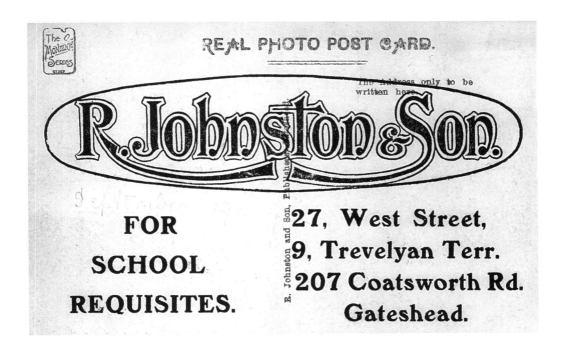

whose work, always of very high quality, covered most of County Durham and the Tyne-Wear region. The Newcastle Central Library holds an excellent archive of their work.

One final point about the postcards is, of course, the fact that many of those available to us had written messages on them. One of the most pleasurable aspects of working with old cards is the opportunity it affords to people as inquisitive as the authors to pry into the lives of other people through the medium of their scribbled messages to friends, family and colleagues. So that is just what we have done.

Now a brief word about bias, manipulation and unreliability.

There is no doubt about the value of photographs in revealing aspects of life and labour in a graphic form in a way which cannot be matched by documentary archives, however detailed. However, while 'the camera cannot lie' that does not mean that photographs must always be accepted fully at face value as a truthful record. There are two causes of uncertainty; technological limitations and human manipulation, conscious or unconscious.

The most prevalent technical problems are to do with exposure times and lighting. Now in fact photographers could achieve very fast exposure times by the end of the nineteenth century so that the day was gone when subjects of portrait photos had to sit still and rigid for several minutes. However, one of the blacksmith's photographs illustrates in a small way the sort of problem which could still arise with a set-piece photograph. More significant was the problem of interior lighting. By the turn of the century all of the basic inventions and innovations had been made. However, there are still remarkably few interior views of school classrooms or shops or public houses. There are some in this collection but they are prominent for their rarity!

Far more subtle and diverse are the methods of human manipulation. There are no examples here – apart possibly from a rowing boat at Fatfield – of the sort of scissors and paste and re-photographing of composite images which did happen in many well authenticated cases (one of the most famous Sunderland photographers was undeniably guilty of such trickery). There are lots of examples of photographs which obviously meant something to the photographer but have no supporting captions or details of any sort leaving the viewer to impose his own interpretation. We do exactly the same thing today so can hardly complain. There are many examples of un-captioned photographs in this collection where the authors have had to use their own imagination and 'on-the-ground' knowledge. In a few cases we have just confessed ignorance quite blatantly!

Equally the process of selection which goes on in choosing subjects for photographs can be misleading, not necessarily intentionally. There tends to be a preponderance of novelty snaps like the Washington village blacksmith for example, but at a time when such scenes were already becoming unusual enough to capture them again and again! Scenes associated with holidays and happy times tend to attract photographs. So there are lots of the famous Girdle Cake Cottage whose life as a riverside café is now very distant but which lingers on in folk memory to this day. Other such photographs include carnivals, anniversaries and other celebrations. Dramatic events such as the Glebe Colliery disaster referred to earlier also attracted photographers.

There is also a form of falsification which is referred to by one of the Washington sources quoted here. It is clear that the pictures of school classes were often preceded by the dressing up of children from a school chest and that the children were sometimes positioned in such a way to give a better impression of appearance. This is innocent and understandable enough, but it is still misleading.

On the other hand there were those scenes which did not attract photographers because they were too common-place to warrant it. That excludes most of life as it was lived in colliery villages in fact! A nice example of this is the absence of photographs of back lanes and back yards although they were important places for recreation and work (especially for women doing their washing). There are a couple of such scenes here, and one of them actually displays a tin bathtub as well! They are so unusual that you wonder why they were taken. Film was expensive after all. Also if one was to go by these photographs – mostly taken by men – you would imagine that women did not figure so much in colliery life and you gain little impression of the sort of routine household life which revolved around them. Everyday ongoing life is not lived through a lens. The use made of cameras is spasmodic and selective.

These are some examples of the way in which you need to be cautious and to ask questions as you look at photographs from the past. Of course the sorts of selection and misrepresentation referred to above continue still, and on a vast scale. Photographers still refuse to scribble down captions for family snaps, since of course they know who the subjects are and where the photograph was taken. They still insist on specialising in happy family holiday and 'day out' snaps on golden sunny days rather than, for example, 'a family row' or 'stripping the anaglypta in the living room' or 'doing the ironing' or 'in the rain at Seaburn' or 'at the check-out at Asda at 5.00pm.' Pictures of the atypical, unusual and 'one-off' subjects proliferate rather than the common-place ones of typical scenes and life today.

Pity the poor historian of the future!!

Despite all these flaws and reservations we hope you enjoy this collection of postcards and photographs.

ALONG THE RIVER

The best place to start our exploration of Washington is along the river and riverside. It was here that the first industrial community developed on the basis of pits at Fatfield and Biddick and the keel traffic which supplied coal to the colliers waiting in the harbour at Sunderland. Indeed this was the origin of the early economic growth of Sunderland. The river is tidal up to beyond Biddick so we can follow the tide down. The name of the Wear incidentally may be derived from the Germanic wasser, or water, as with the River Weser. This journey will take us out of Washington because it will end at the Hylton Ferry. On the way we glance at Botany Bay, peer at a mock Roman bridge overlooked by a mock Greek temple and encounter the versatile Stephensons. We can stop off at the renowned Girdle Cake Cottage for tea and scones.

Fatfield Bridge from Worm Hill

Leading downhill to the bridge is Beatrice Terrace. Also on the far side of the bridge are the terraces of East Bridge Street and West Bridge Street. Here can be seen the rear of the Biddick Inn. Also across the river can be seen the area known as Wagon Hill until 1921 when it was renamed Mount Pleasant. Chartershaugh Bridge, opened in 1975, is just off to the right of the picture.

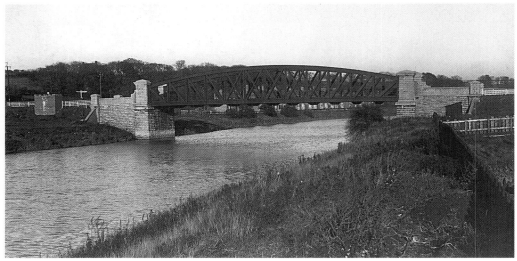

Fatfield Bridge

The main girders are of wrought iron and are 155 feet long. They rest on abutments of solid masonry. The total cost, including the approaches, amounted to £8,000. The bridge was opened by the Earl of Durham on 29th January, 1890. It carried the main road from Washington to Houghton-le-Spring.

Fatfield Bridge from upstream

The postmark on this card seems to be 19th May, 1903. The message reads: 'Dear B. I arrived home safe. It has been raining but I hope the weather improves so as to be able to go out. This is a view of a little place not far off Hylton. You go to it by river. I would not care if me and you were going tomorrow. We would enjoy ourselves. Will send a letter later. X. W.L. (with love !)'.

The B. in receipt of the exclamation-marked love was a Miss B. Dixon, 106 Oakland Road, Hillsborough, Sheffield. The rowing boat image seems to have been superimposed on the picture.

East Bridge Street and Penshaw Staithes
This view is taken from the north end of the Fatfield Bridge. Part of the East Bridge Street is to the right with the adjacent houses (now demolished) of Penshaw Staithes. The waste heap of North Biddick

Colliery can be seen above the trees in the centre left. In the eighteenth and early nineteenth centuries Biddick had a bad reputation for lawlessness. It was the home of keelmen and miners who were more than a match for the forces of law and order or for the gentlemen of the press gang. Technically speaking the keelmen were exempted from impressment into naval service and were eligible for exemption certificates. On more than one occasion the press gang was repelled with serious casualties. Indeed Biddick had such a bad name that it is suggested that this is why it was known as Botany Bay.

The Ferry Boat Inn
This is John Todd's Ferry Boat Inn. Such riverside inns catered very much for the keelmen in the days of the keel trade. Each inn usually had a room furnished for them. The 'keelers room' would have its floors dusted with powdered sandstone and there were benches where the keelmen could rest between the loading of their keels and the time of the tide. There were many such inns. They included the Peareth Arms, the Spotted Cow, the Punch Bowl, the Havelock Arms, the Biddick Inn, the Bird in the Bush, the William IV, the Woodside Inn, the Oddfellows and the Bluebell Inn. Nowadays the survivors cater for weekend walkers and cyclists.

Flannigan's Temperance Bar

The sign reads 'Flannigan's Temperance Bar and Tea Rooms. Parties are catered for'. Whatever the occupants preceding Flannigan's were licensed to sell has been deleted. This was located on the south side of the river downstream from Fatfield Bridge. These non-alcohol meeting places were a reaction against the problem of drink. They were the early equivalent of the coffee bar.

Penshaw Staithes

The staithes stood at the far end of East Bridge Street. They were the terminus of the waggonway which led down from Penshaw and carried coal. Penshaw Monument is in the dim distance to the far left.

Girdle Cake Cottage viewed from the river

This scene was a very popular one. The cottage was situated on the north bank of the river. It was a popular venue throughout the later 19th Century and into the early 1930s because afternoon teas and other refreshments were served there. To the right of it were coal pits. It was demolished in the 1930s but the memory lingers on. People would travel upstream from Sunderland by boat have their tea and then return on the tide.

Girdle Cake Cottage

The cottage was demolished in 1932 by a Mr. Booth who was a bricklayer. The pantiles were used on another cottage which he was building. The last resident was Tom Davison, miner and fiddler. It was replaced on this site by Newall's Pumping Station. The ferry boat crossed from here to the Bird in the Bush on the other side of the river.

VICTORIA BRIDGE WASHINGTON

The Victoria Viaduct

The postmark date is the 6th July, 1904. The message reads 'This is the Wear, the river where B.K. & I used to swim. Am having a very decent time & am sorry have to leave. T.P.' It is addressed to a Miss W. Weatherdale, 27 Alderson Street, West Hartlepool.

The bridge carried the London and North Eastern Railway over the river. It was originally designed for the Durham Junction Railway which was intended to take the coal trade from the Houghton-le-Spring and Hartlepool areas and redirect it to the Tyne as part of the Great Railway Game which excited speculators in the 1830s and 1840s. The Durham Junction joined the Stanhope and Tyne Railway at Washington. In fact it was swallowed up in 1843 by the network of George Hudson, the Bill Gates (and eventually the Robert Maxwell) of his day.

The bridge was designed by T.E.Harrison. It was patterned on the Roman bridge at Alcantara in Spain. It was opened officially on the Coronation Day of Queen Victoria although it did not actually open to traffic until 1839. It has a length of 270 yards. It consists of four semi-circular arches of 160 feet, 144 feet and two of 100 feet span. Together with three arches of 20 feet span at each end. The stone used was freestone from Penshaw. The outer quoins are of Aberdeen granite. Its length is 810 feet. It is 21 feet wide. Its height from ground to parapet top is 157 feet. It was built at a cost of £35,000. Pevsner, the author and editor of the definitive series of county guides to buildings of historical and architectural interest, says of the bridge: 'The general style of the design is at once simple and grand. It is both elegant and imposing in appearance without superfluous ornament, and in this respect it harmonises with the surrounding scenery.' He also marvels: 'Is there any other place where one can stand beneath a Roman 'viaduct' and see a Greek 'temple' near by?'

The Victoria Viaduct
The bridge carried the main railway line from Newcastle to London originally. The main line was re-routed via Durham in 1872. The bridge was closed in 1991 although the last train over it was in 1993.

Victoria Bridge Ferry
The ferry at Victoria Bridge with North Biddick Colliery miners, *circa* 1920.

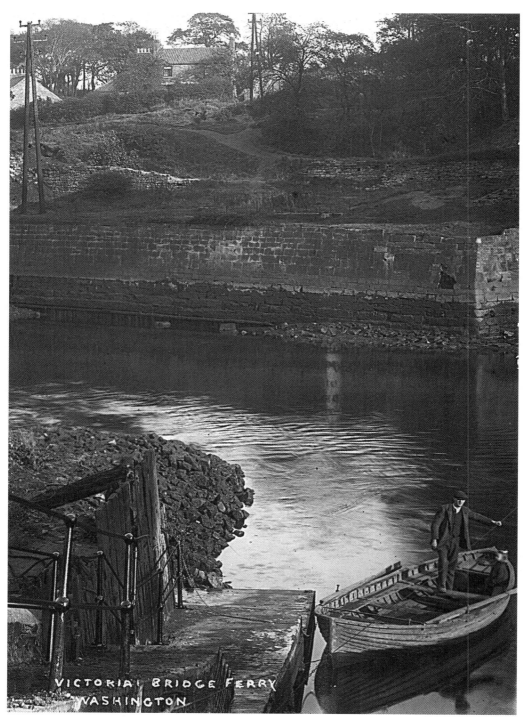

Victoria Bridge Ferry

Cox Green from the north east

There is no address but the message reads 'Dear Laura. Wishing you the best of health, mummy will write soon. Love Lucy XXXXXX'. Lucy didn't post it for some reason though, or she may have posted it in an envelope as was sometimes done. The delicate First World War flowery and paper-lace postcards, for example, were usually sent in envelopes to protect them

The ferry steps at Cox Green are very clear. The boat is probably the rowing boat ferry between Cox Green and the Washington staithes which was operated for many years by the Frost family. In the earlier days it was a very profitable enterprise. In the period from the 1890s to 1914 it cost (returns) $1\frac{1}{2}$d for adults, 1d for children and 2d for bicycles. Most Cox Green villagers had no choice because many of them worked at the Washington Chemical Works, housewives shopped at Washington and pensioners went there to collect their money when pensions were introduced. But in later years the ferry tended to be less in operation because the ferryman got another job! Since it was operated under Royal Charter there were grounds for complaint. However the Charter could not be found. A letter was sent to the Queen though. As a result in January 1956 Mr. Frost, the operator of the day, laid down (or hung up) his oars.

This view is from the Barmston area. The historian Fordyce had this to say of Barmston in 1857: 'Barmston is situated along the Wear, nearly opposite to Offerton, five miles west of Sunderland. Here are a spade and shovel manufactory, a blacksmiths shop and a ferry boat on the river.' Fordyce doesn't do it justice though. There was a very wide variety of industries or industrial remains there in the 1850s including timber yards, coke ovens, a brewery, brickyards, old pit shafts, obsolete waggonways and old sandstone quarries. Along the north bank are the Barmston ferry houses and then the cottages of the staithmen. You can see smoke rising from the chimneys of the houses on the Cox Green side. Nearly all of these cottages would have relied on the free coal allowances from the collieries.

A view across the Wear from Cox Green
This is a view from the west of Cox Green across the river. There are four men in the boat to the left.

In 1812 there were 23 collieries in the two miles from Lambton Park to Washington Staithes. There were more than 300 keels engaged in carrying coal to the colliers at Sunderland. Jackie Stephenson of the local Barmston family claimed that he had often crossed the river by stepping from keel to keel as they passed along (he was also renowned as an inventive spinner of tales!)

A view of the Wear at Cox Green
The view from downstream of the Victoria Viaduct at Cox Green.

Cox Green Ferry Landing

A full frontal view of the ferry landing with the Barmston ferry houses to the right. Barmston is written in old records variously as Berneston or Bermeston. It probably derives from Beorns-tun. Beorn was a common Anglo-Saxon personal name. The suffix – tun means settlement and is the origin of the word town.

At Barmston incidentally lived the famous Stephenson family for about three hundred years from the late 16th Century. They were keel builders, farmers, shipbuilders, shovel makers and iron smiths. They made iron work for wooden sailing ships. Some of their iron work was on display at the Great Exhibition in 1851. Their factory was at Barmston Forge where they had a water mill. The 1871 Census gives details of a street of houses called Barmston Forge, and records a 'Mr. John Stephenson, manufacturer of spades, shovels and metal implements.' The last Stephenson was Jackie who died in 1904. After his death the house and mill were demolished. The site of Barmston Forge is now part of the Washington Wildfowl and Wetlands Centre.

It would not be right to pass this scene without reference to the most famous ferryman of Barmston – the Earl of Perth. It is claimed that the sixth Earl of Perth, James Drummond who fled from Culloden's bloody field, took a ship (*The Mars*) for France, landed at South Shields and settled at the notorious Biddick (indeed 'Go to Biddick' was a condemnatory dismissal in the 19th Century) in the abode of a collier called Jack Armstrong. He married Armstrong's daughter in 1749. Then he moved to a cottage called the Boat House on the North Biddick side of the river to the south of the Girdle Cake House. He had charge of the ferry boat as occupant of that cottage. Then catastrophe! In the Great Flood of 17th November 1771 the Boat House was washed away, and with it went the wooden box including all of the family documents including the Ducal Patent of Nobility. That sounds a bit like some sort of bogus insurance claim. However the consequence was that after the death of the Earl/ferryman in 1782 the claim was carried on by his descendants, but to no avail. His grandson is buried at Penshaw under a stone (near the churchyard gate) which bears the inscription 'Also the above Thomas Drummond. The Rightful Heir to the Earldom of Perth. Who died Novr. 18th, 1873, aged 81 years'.

Cox Green Footbridge under construction in 1958
The view is towards the north west. The footbridge is partially completed. In the background are the Barmston Ferry Houses, Chemical Works and Waste Heap.

A water mill
This card is addressed to Mrs. G. Eley at Usworth House, Springwell, Gateshead. The (rain smudged) message reads:
'We are sorry that we can not get to see you on Sunday but perhaps we will see you sometime soon. I hope you are all well and liking your new home. We do miss you all. Kindest regards. S. A. Newton.'

This is an overshot water wheel. It may well be the water mill of Jackie Stephenson.

Wear Water Cottage
This view is from the south side of the river. The date may be 18th May, 1908. The card is addressed to Miss M. Jamieson, 6 Park View, Roker, Sunderland. The message reads: 'Dear Sister. Mother could not come down today as she was papering the room. But she was very sorry. I will write & remain your loving sister.'

The Hylton Rowing Ferry
This view of the rowing boat ferry is from the south side of the river. The Shipwrights can be seen at the bottom of Ferryboat Lane. It is approximately 350 years old. At various times the building has accommodated a ship's chandler, a post office and a fire station. It was also a coaching house. At one time there were some 14 inns and public houses from here to the Alexandra Bridge serving the needs of the work-force from the shipyards as well as local residents.

The Ferry, Hylton   Photo by H. Hall 3

The Hylton Ferry Boats
Here can be seen the two ferries. There was a rowing boat ferry and there was a rope governed ferry used to transport carriages and wagons. There are eight people in the boat including one oarsman. Policemen seem to have been trained to stand and stare at cameras judging from their prevalence in photographs of the day!

The daughters of the Hylton Ferryman
This seems to have been taken at the allotments near Hylton. This family had the Hylton Ferry. These are the daughters of the ferryman. This is a lovely portrait postcard. The whites of the eyes of the sedentary sister have been exaggerated though. The fence in the background includes sections of a bacon box.

SECTION TWO

FATFIELD AND BIDDICK

In the next three sections we explore the various village communities of Washington before moving on to pick out some themes. Fatfield and Biddick have already been encountered in the section on the river and riverside so here we move away from the river a little. We also take in Penshaw Hill and Penshaw Monument here because they do dominate this area so much. The name Biddick first appears in the Boldon Book as Bedic. In other records it appears as Biddich, Bedyk and Bidwich. It probably means either 'the dwelling of Bida or Beda' or 'the ditch or dyke of Bida or Beda'. The inn sign of The Biddick is, therefore, not unreasonably a labourer digging a ditch. Even then South Biddick must have been a sizeable village because it was recorded that the villeins 'provide 160 men for reaping in the autumn and 36 carts for carting corn to Houghton.'

Washington Lane, Fatfield

Washington Lane in Fatfield
The postmark date is 24th March, 1905.

23

The Havelock Arms and River Wear Terrace
This will be the late 1960s or the 1970s. The view is south west from Worm Hill to the gable end of the Havelock Arms. Behind are houses and shops on the south side of Bonemill Lane (River View Terrace). The river is in the centre background with the Chatershaugh shaft of Harraton Colliery to the right. It is ironic that so many public houses in Britain are named after General Havelock because he was not only the officer commanding the relief column at Lucknow in 1857 during the Indian Mutiny he was also a prominent advocate of temperance in the British army! He was born in Sunderland of course, and is the subject of one of the three personal monuments in Mowbray Park.

A view up Bonemill Lane to St George's, Fatfield
This is a good view of Bonemill Lane. To the left is the waggonway which carried coal from Harraton Colliery to the Chatershaugh Staithes for shipment to Sunderland. Fatfield School was built in 1876. St George's Church to the left rear was built in 1879. The school is encountered again, with some of its children, in a later section.

A general view of Fatfield

This interesting picture shows a very sizeable community living in rows of colliery terraced housing. The riverside area of Washington saw the first industrial communities because of the pits sunk in Fatfield and Barmston, and because of the keel trade and shipyards. In fact it is claimed that the first steamship built on the Wear was engined at Biddick. Some of the earliest waggonways in the region were built at Fatfield and Biddick. As early as 1693 Thomas Allen of Flatts Colliery built a line which was later extended to Pelton Fell and Pelton Moor. Another was built close to it in 1710 by Dean Hedworth, and that ran eventually to Ouston and Beamish. On the south of the river three waggonways were built by the Lambtons before 1737. It has been calculated that by 1787 there were no fewer than fifteen lines carrying coal to keels within no more than two miles.

Worm Hill

Before the First World War the predominant form of housing in these mining settlements was the terraced rows built by colliery owners. After 1919 council housing was introduced in the area but Fatfield retained its terraced rows much later.

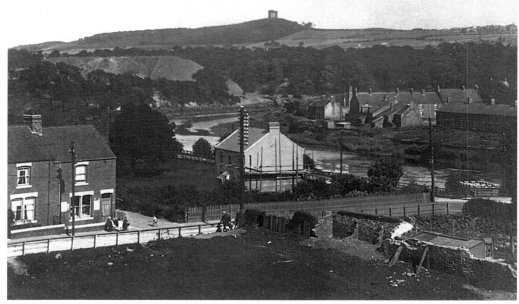

A view across Biddick to Penshaw Hill

This is a superb view dominated by a natural hill and an artificial hill. The former is Penshaw Hill. The latter is the spoil heap of North Biddick Colliery. It is very easy to forget the extent of industrialisation along a riverside which is nowadays a pleasant rural walk.The name of Penshaw Hill is an interesting exercise in place-names. There are many different spellings: Pencher (1190), Penchare (1472), Pensher (1649), Painshea (1760), Pencher (1764), Painshay (1783), Painshard (1783), Penshew (1803), Painsher (1850), Penshaw (1895).

Whatever the spelling the origin seems to be Pen = hill and Shaw = wood ie. The Wooded Hill. The redundant word 'Hill' seems to have been added late in the day by the tidy-minded military cartographers of the Ordnance Survey.

On top of Penshaw Monument

Penshaw Monument

The monument is the subject of several controversies and curious stories. One is that it was actually built in recognition of the second Earl of Durham, the second son of the first Earl and a very popular (but living) landowner. It is also claimed locally that the monument is incomplete and was supposed to have a rider on horseback on the top. An extreme version of this is that the statue of the Marquess of Londonderry in Durham market square was meant to go there. Strangest of all is the legend that the cost was paid by land tenants grateful because the Earl refused to raise his rents unlike other landowners, but then raised them when he saw the money which could be afforded for this frivolity! In fact this latter is exactly the same story as that attached to the Alnwick Tenantry Column erected in the years of agricultural depression after Waterloo.

The architects of Penshaw Monument were the omnipresent John and Benjamin Green. The foundation stone was laid on the 28th August, 1844. It cost £3000 to build; the money being raised by private subscription. It was made of stone from the Marsden Quarry of the Marquis of Londonderry. It was modelled – loosely – on the Theseion at Athens. It is 100 feet long by 53 feet wide. The Theseion is four feet longer and eight feet narrower. The Greek pattern has 54 columns, each 3 feet 4 inches thick, while Penshaw Monument has 18 which are twice as thick. Apart from that they are more or less identical!

The monument was erected in memory of John George Lambton, the 1st Earl of Durham. There was a plaque on the monument originally which referred to the 'Distinguished Talents and Exemplary Private Virtues of the Earl'. He died in 1840 of tuberculosis (as did four of his children). He was a leader of the campaign for parliamentary reform which culminated in the Great Reform Act of 1832, and was the author of the Durham Report on Canada which is regarded as the foundation document of the Commonwealth of Nations. That at least is the official version. We'll present the less attractive version of him later on!

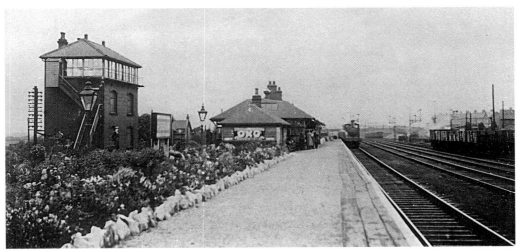

Penshaw Station
The date is 22nd September 1924. The original main Durham-Sunderland route was via Pittington. In 1931 that line was ended at Pittington and the main route went via Penshaw. Then that line was closed to passengers on the 5th May, 1964. It continued to be used for freight until 1967.

Fatfield War Memorial

There is no room here to do justice to the legend of the Lambton Worm. However it is only one of a dozen or more in the north of England alone, and often with common features. In reality the origin of the legends probably resides with the pagan practice of sacrificing nubile women to crocodiles in order to stimulate the life-giving rains – not in Fatfield of course, but in eastern countries whence the (embroidered) stories were brought by crusaders and other travellers. There is also an element of tall story telling and the need to stimulate the tourist trade. In fact if you wander along the river bank beside West Bridge Street you will, oddly enough, find a stone crocodile. There are other fanciful theories about this legend. They include the idea that the slaying of the dragon is really commemorative of the defeating (or wishful defeating) of the Viking invaders in their dragon-ships. There is also a view that the stories could have been developed to explain the skeleton remains of dinosaurs. Apart from the Worm connection the hill was once home to fairies. They were – so it is said – frightened away by the noise and pollution of the mining. However it is claimed that they can still be seen at midnight when mid-Summer commences. Presumably that depends on how much you've had to drink at The Biddick.

The War Memorial no longer stands on the top of the hill but is at the base next to the water trough dedicated by the former Harraton District Council to the legend of the Lambton Worm. True believers obviously, or with cash to spare at the end of the financial year!

Chatershaugh Bonfire
The original correct spelling of this place-name seems to be Chartershaugh but it is invariably spelt Chatershaugh so we have not deviated. The suffix 'haugh' means meadow but the origin of Chater or Charter is not clear. It is to be hoped that the man with the cigarette remembers where he is in time!

South View in North Biddick

North Biddick Hall from the west

Biddick Hall originally belonged to the Hilton family. William Hilton was in the second vessel of the Pilgrim Fathers to the New World in 1621. The modern Hall was the home of the Cook family in the later 19th Century. In fact it became better known as Cook's Hall. Joseph Cook founded the Washington Ironworks after the end of a partnership with John Nicholson which had premises on the Wear bank at North Biddick. Nicholson continued in the original premises until 1900. J. and R. Cook's went on to become a very large concern specialising in all sorts of colliery ironwork and equipment. The Hall was demolished in 1966 largely due to subsidence.

North Biddick Hall. The west and south sides
The postmark date is 24th December, 1903. The card is addressed to Mrs. T. Boswell Watson, Great South Hawker, Woldingham, Surrey. The message reads: 'With best love and every good wish for Christmas and a Bright New Year from all. Blanche'. There were actually postal deliveries on Christmas Day. Postcards with that postmark date tend to be quite valuable.

WASHINGTON VILLAGE

The old agrarian village of Washington is the historical focus of the wider community. It was first mentioned in the Boldon Book as being in the ownership of one William of Hartburn:

'William of Hartburn has Washington except the church and the land belonging to the church in exchange for the township of Hartburn to which on account of this he renounced all claims and he pays £4 and goes on the Great Chase with 2 greyhounds. And when the common feudal aid comes he ought to give one mark in addition to the aid.'

A witch, a ghost (of a sort), a highwayman and the Statue of Liberty are encountered in this quick tour.

Village Lane, Washington

Village Lane
The postmark date is 22nd August 1904. The card is addressed to a Mrs. W. Barratt, 7 Dudley Way, West Bromwich. The message is not very legible but the essence is that this card is being sent in exchange for other 'very pretty' cards received from a friend.

The Black Bush Inn
The staff and customers outside the public house. It is now the Poacher's
Pocket (which commemorates one of the less official industries in this area). It
was situated on the south side of Village Lane. The proprietor then was
G. Nevin.

Old Washington.

Washington Village Centre
This is an Auty Series postcard. The date is 1907. The famous blacksmiths was
in the hands of a family called Dobson for many years.

Washington Village Centre
Note the water cart which was used to dampen down the roads in hot weather.

TRINITY CHURCH, WASHINGTON. (852)

Trinity Church
The postmark date is 1916. The card is addressed to Mrs. F.Hubbard, 85 Knighton Fields Road, Leicester. It was sent by a soldier. The message reads: 'Sat.Morning. Dear Ma, Pa, and Lily. Thanks for your letter and your kind offer to send me anything. I have finished a parcel off that Sally & Bert sent me; and it was a treat after some of our rough rations. Some baked currant pudding was very nice. This is the church I went to last Sunday. And all soldiers there were given a supper when we came out, in the schools. We had tea & coffee & sandwiches & buttered buns. As much as we could eat. Hoping all are quite well. Frank.'

Trinity Church and the War Memorial This is one of many postcards in the Monarch Series by R. Johnston and Sons.

Trinity Church & War Memorial, Washington. 3317

In 1696 a woman called Jane Atkinson was buried in the churchyard. Local legend has it that she had actually been drowned in the village pond. She was, so it is said, tied in a sack and thrown into a pond when an outbreak of cattle disease was blamed on her. As evidence of this quaint story it is claimed that the register entry says 'witch' by her name. In fact it says 'practitioner' which suggests that she had some sort of claim to medical expertise rather than the Black Arts. The war memorial is on the site of the old pond. In fact Mrs Atkinson, a woman who was a pew-holder so must have been someone of means, was buried respectably in the graveyard. So the story is wrong on just about every count but such tales add a nice human touch don't they?

A Memorial Service
This view must have been taken from the front of the blacksmiths. This is one of a set of postcards taken seconds apart. It is interesting to compare them as the group breaks up. The children are far more concerned about the photographer than the solemnities of the service.

The Old Hall, Washington. 10159

Washington Old Hall

This is a R. Johnston (Gateshead) Monarch Series postcard. The card has no date or address. The message was written however: 'This old hall is now closed. We had many American visitors to see it last year. Thought these views would be of interest to you.'

It is a good view of the Old Hall (not to be confused with Washington Hall). The original was built in the 12th Century by William de Wessynton. Then in the 14th Century the family moved on eventually to settle in Northamptonshire. John Washington emigrated to America in the 1650s and George Washington was descended from him. In the 18th Century the hall itself was let out to tenants. It gradually decayed. In Whellan's Directory (1894) it was described as 'fast falling into decay'. In 1936 it was actually declared unfit for human habitation. By the efforts of a local preservation committee it was saved and restored, then opened to the public in 1955 in a ceremony held on the 28th September. In 1957 it was transferred to the National Trust. Structurally it is a nice example of a medium sized early 17th Century H Plan house of local sandstone and with a symmetrical front towards the church.

Postcards

The majority of the postcards which survive in collections today (and probably in private hands) seem to have been sent to women. Or it may be that women are more likely to retain them.

A view of Washington Village from the churchyard

There was a very curt message. All it says is 'This is the old blacksmiths shop'. To the right is the Cross Keys Inn of Mr James Dunwoodie. There is a nice view from the church over the gravestones and the blacksmith's. Associated with the latter is the story of Robert Hazlitt, highwayman.

It is said that in 1770 a grey horse being shod at the blacksmiths was identified as that of a local highwayman called Hazlitt who had been involved in a robbery at Gateshead. It appears that a sharp sighted pot-boy had noted the number plate and sporting stripes and reported the sighting to the authorities. Hazlitt was arrested on the basis of that evidence then hanged and caged on a gibbet at the foot of the Long-Bank Wrekenton! And all for the want of a horse shoe nail!

Parish Church, Washington

This postcard was sent from The Manse, Washington on 21st July 1933.

The Village Green

The Washington Arms can be seen here. It was originally the Three Horse Shoes. Later it became the Smiths Arms, then the Commercial Hotel and then (now) the Washington Arms. So for those people who complain about the tendency to rename inns 'Dirty Murphy's' or 'Rosie's Bar' and regard it as a betrayal of the past and 'our heritage' this might be an object lesson in changing with the times and the need to adapt to different clienteles!

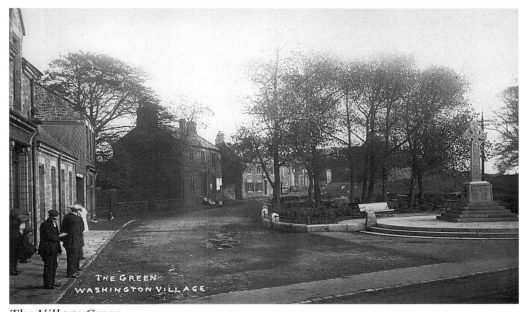

The Village Green

The old police station is the building in the centre. It had accommodation for a sergeant and six constables. To the left is the Cross Keys and then a shop. The police station later became a guest house (which in a sense it already was!). The shop became Washington Green library, opened in 1930.

Washington Green Library and the Mobile Library
The Mobile Library served an invaluable purpose in an area of scattered village communities, and its visits were quite a high point.

Washington Warship Week Pageant
This was in March 1942. One of the objectives of the parade was to raise funds for the National Savings Warship Week. This view is looking northwards from the crossroads near the Cross Keys towards Spout Lane. The leading vehicle has Emily Rodham dressed as the Statue of Liberty. Later on she became Mrs. Forte. The sign says '£ s d Lease Lend'. In fact the weeks efforts raised £57,000 to pay for a Trawler Mine Sweeper called *The Sarabande*.

A Milk Float
Milk is still being supplied by the jug here judging from the boy to the right. Heaven knows how people continued to survive in these appalling conditions! We have the security of Health and Safety and EU regulations around us now though.

Hunters Bedford Bus
This service ran from Waterloo Usworth Colliery to Waterside Washington Staithes. This picture shows it at Wilden Terrace.

Council Steam-rollers

This and the next four photographs are taken from a series which seem to have been taken by a District Council employee in the 1950s judging from the preponderance of Council vehicles and staff. Various Urban District Council vehicles can be seen here standing near the village green.

Council dust-bin wagon

The two Council employees are obviously subscribers to the 'if we stand and watch long enough!' school of thought. In the background is the waste heap of F Pit.

The Washington Fire Brigade

The Hostel Garage
Cars and a bus standing outside the Hostel Garage.

Bambrough's Garage

Biddick Row
The date is 28th April 1905. The card was addressed to Mrs. McKenzie, 16 Hedley Street, Wallsend. The message reads: 'Lizzie. Polly and I will leave here with the eleven train in the morning. Effie.'

The Avenue
The date is not clear. The card was addressed to a Miss S. Turnbull, 53 Percy Street, Whitley Bay. The message reads: 'D.S. Received your card & pleased to hear you are having a good time. Your stay is getting very short now. Expect Connie is having a rare time. Trust you received Mothers card. With love Millie.'

Municipal and Spout Lanes
The water for Washington came from the Mount to Blue House fields, to F Pit and then to the village. It was known as the Spout. Beyond Washington it passed down to the Washington Chemical Works and the Washington Staithes.

Station Road
The post office was one of the buildings on the right.

Washington Post Office
There is a house being built just along the road. This is a good point to stop and consider the meaning of the place-name Washington. It appears in various guises in old records. In the Boldon Book (1183) it is Wessyntona. Variants include Quessington, Wessingatun, Wasshington and Westington. The most likely origin is 'the farm of the sons of Wassa or Wessa'. It could be derived from the Old Norse Wazwere which means marsh or water, or Vaskjarr which means a wet marsh. There is no doubt that this whole area will have been very wet.

Station Road
This and the next view are both of Station Road which led to Washington
Station. Leading from it was a network of terraces.

Havannah Terrace back lane
This could be a back lane anywhere. Considering how many people spent so
much time in the back lane it is surprising that there are so few photographs –
but that, perversely, is the very reason. Back lanes were a God-send for
parents. Children would spend many hours playing in the back lane and out of
harms way. Housewives used it for hanging out their washing. The games
played by children were actually seasonal to an extent which they are not
today. It was skipping, 'alleys' (marbles for posh folk!) and chuckstones (or
knucklestones) in the Summer, then tops and whips and conkers in the
Autumn, sledging in the Winter and ball games (and hula hoops when they
joined the repertoire) in Spring.

Derwent Terrace
One of the several terraces which make up Station Road. On the right hand
side is Glen Terrace.

Derwent and Glen Terraces

Emmerson Terrace
The date may be 1920. The card is addressed to Miss Nellie Coppock,
33 Hazelwood Road, Nottingham. It reads:
'This is our home for the time being. The bottom house. Weather is poor but
not troubling us. Going to Sunderland today. Keep smiling. Daddy.'

WASHINGTON. 1027

Station Road
This is quite an old scene, the postmark date is 1907. The building on the left
is now Westwood Club. The house on the right is the 'Red House'. The road is
not made up. The message reads: 'Well Dear Mother. Just a line hoping it will
find yourself & all at home in the best of health. The largest house is ours.
With love & heaps of kisses! Your loving & affectionate daughter. May.'

Black Fell Camp

This was a full-time army base during the Second World War. Later it was used by the Territorial Army. The camp stood on the site which is now occupied by Dickens' Hypermarket. Before Dickens' there was a RCA record factory there. It was one of the suppliers of Elvis Presley records and was almost overwhelmed by the demand which resulted from the death of 'The King'. There seem to be no photographs available of any of the many men who did their training at the camp.

Black Fell is no stranger to warfare. It was here that was fought the battle of Shadon's Hill (or Gateside Fell) in 1068 where William of Normandy defeated a combined force of Scots and Danes and Northern English rebels led by Edgar the Atheling and King Malcolm of Scotland. This was followed by his devastation of the northern region to prevent a recurrence. So the area is not mentioned in the Domesday Book although it does figure in the Boldon Book of 1183.

This was also the scene of meetings of miners addressed by Tommy Hepburn in 1831-32 in his fight for higher wages and better conditions and a shorter working day.

NEW WASHINGTON, WASHINGTON STATION AND THE USWORTHS

Towards the end of the 19th Century the mining communities of Washington and Usworth Colliery began to merge to create New Washington. Whellan, in his Directory, described this development as follows:

'A straggling village partly in Washington, and partly in Usworth. It comprises several good shops, and has lately been improved by a terrace of neat stone houses. It is situated one and a quarter miles north of Washington township. Many of the inhabitants are employed at Usworth Colliery, and Usworth Station is situated a mile to the east!' (1894)

Front Street, New Washington
This is an Auty Series postcard. Walter Willson's is to the left in the mid-ground of the picture.

Front Street, New Washington

Postcards were used for fairly routine messages in a way that we do not use them today. In this case it was from Usworth Colliery to New Washington. The postmark date seems to be 1913. The card is addressed to Miss Maria Gates, 14 Ferry Street, Bear Park Colliery, Nr. Durham. The message reads:

'Dear Maria. I am now sending you a card. I was very sorry on Saturday when I came away that I could not come down your street and say good morning to you all as we had very little time and my parcels were so heavy. I hope you will both write back to me and let me know how you are keeping. From Mary. 27 Single Row, Usworth Colliery.'

The New Inn, Front Street, New Washington circa 1914

The rather grand and elaborate building with the cupola is the New Inn. It became the New Tavern – and looks very much the same. This is clearly at a time when the roads were unmade. On the left – the name can just be made out – is the shop of R.Elliott, grocer and draper. Elliott's later became Anderson's the drapers and then a branch of Lloyds Bank.

New Washington.

The New Inn and R. Elliott's shop
Another Auty Series postcard. The New Inn is to the right. R.Elliott's shop is to
the left with the ever-present sign 'Frys Pure Cocoa'.

A typical Washington back lane
Note the tin bath hanging up on the wall. Bath night was Friday night in the
days before easily accessible piped hot water. The ritual took place in front of
the coal fire. First the girls and then the boys. In the first edition of this book
we did not know the exact location of this lane. It has now been identified as
Hunters Terrace, Springwell.

Co-operative Terrace, Washington. 3320

Co-operative Terrace, New Washington
The Front Street of New Washington is a continuation of Station Road. It is made up of terraces. This is Co-operative Terrace which leads to Hawthorn Terrace beyond.

Brady Square
The woman on the right has a rolled up carpet and looks rather anxious. There is a boy to her right with some sort of hand barrow. The Wills Gold Flake advert was a very prevalent one. This view is looking south across the level crossing. Anderson's (newsagents) is to the left. An early Northern bus is in the centre left. Also to be seen are the gable ends of Albert Place (centre), a Morris Cowley Bullnose (right) and Biddick School in the distance. At Railway Terrace in Brady Square the open level crossing was used by coal trains from F Pit and Glebe Colliery

The Earl of Durham Inn

The Earl of Durham Inn was well positioned to catch trade from the local collieries and chemical works. The first Earl of Durham was a popular figure locally – indeed the Lambtons as a family have always enjoyed considerable popularity in the region. The 'populist' view of the financing of Penshaw Monument is that it was built with the pennies of loyal labourers and colliers. On its return in 1840 his body was met by a grieving audience of miners and their families. There is no doubt that 'Squire Lambton' was a popular man despite cynical views as to other motives for being conspicuously present as mourners!

In fact Lambton was unpopular amongst fellow politicians who regarded him as an erratic 'loose cannon', too prone to courting public adulation. He also mixed with some very shady companions who were involved in a grand concept of imperial reform which would, incidentally, benefit their pockets as well. He was sent to Canada partly to get rid of a nuisance and set him an impossible task. The famous report was really a plan to promote emigration to Canada to swamp a troublesome French minority rather than the foundation of a multi-ethnic democratic Commonwealth! A classic example of his manipulating of public image was his claim that he would do the job for expenses only. However these turned out to include a string of racehorses and an orchestra. Here was a man who needed no 'spin doctor', and was quite capable of achieving his own 'make-overs'. Nevertheless he was a talented man who left very positive marks on the British and Imperial political and constitutional scenery and deserved to have inns named after him.

Washington Station circa 1909
On the platform the guard is telling a woman about the leaves on the tracks or about the type of snow being sent nowadays or to buy Rail-track shares!

Frederick Sterling Newall of the Washington Chemical Company set up a wire rope and cable factory near Washington Station in 1887. Amongst other things it made the cable for the transatlantic connection between Britain and America. He also set up what was probably the first aluminium smelting works in the country, and the area around Washington Station became known as Aluminia.

Station Road, Usworth
Station Road is made up of a number of terraces. It was the main road from Washington to the east. It led from New Washington (Concord) to Usworth Station, then the Three Horse Shoes and Sunderland. It became Front Street in New Washington. The shop to the left is a nice example of one of many in the north east which are simply converted houses. The advert seems to be for Pratts Spirit.

Usworth Village

The Red Lion Inn, no longer there, is at the right. Fordyce described the village as follows: 'the village is situated on the declivity of a rocky hill two miles north of Washington and contains two public houses, several mechanics and shopkeepers and a blacksmiths and a chapel belonging to the Wesleyan Methodists'.

High Usworth

The Red Lion Inn was an old one which dated back at least to 1828. It was demolished and the village green now extends over the former site.

Farm buildings at High Usworth
Usworth appears in ancient records as Osaworth, Ousworth and Usworth. It is usually interpreted as 'the enclosed settlement of Osa' or 'Osa's work' or 'the enclosure near the by-road'. If it is the latter the road would have been a Roman road from Usworth to Gateshead.

A view from Usworth House Farm Tithe Barn
Looking south east from the tithe barn.

The Bluebell Inn, High Usworth
This is near the top of Well Bank. The old church school erected by the
benevolence of Susan Peareth in 1814 stood by the right of the inn. She not
only funded this school for poor children but also left a bequest to support
other schools.

A general view from High Usworth

Candy Bank
This is a 1910 scene. This was on the Peareth Hall Road which was the main road from Usworth Village to Springwell.

A show on Usworth Hall Field
The common land in Washington at Washington Moor and Usworth Common was taken possession of by the Lawsons, Musgraves and Shaftoes in 1769-77.

This could be Usworth Flower Show which was held in the field where the present schools are. Races, huge tents with flowers and vegetables, side shows and kite flying competitions attracted the crowds. Possibly the greatest attraction for children was the blue indelible stamp on their hands which was their pass if they wanted to leave the field and return later.

Usworth Hall

This card is dated 23rd December 1905. It is an Auty Series card, and was tinted. It was addressed to Mr and Mrs Price, Shotton Colliery, Castle Eden, Co. Durham. The message is a simple 'Wishing you a Merry Xmas and a Happy New Year. Mount House. Xmas 1905.' The subject of Usworth Hall and Usworth House is confusing so read the next section carefully!

There is a need to distinguish between Usworth House (or Peareth Hall) and Usworth Hall (or Usworth Place). This is actually Usworth House shown here. Usworth Hall (or Place), a 'good stone building' built by Captain Bernard Shaw of the 2nd Foot Regiment, was used as Development Corporation Offices (from 1965) having served as residence of the Usworth Colliery owners then as NCB Group offices. It is on the Stephenson Industrial Estate. It is a plain building of *circa* 1800 with five bays, and two storeys in ashlar.

Usworth Village originally belonged to the Barons Hilton (supposedly a pre-1066 Saxon title). One of the family is said to have saved the people of Usworth from the Black Death in 1349 by burning down the village! New cottages had, however, been built but the people were not prepared to move until they were expelled. Incidentally Catherine Carr the wife of the famous rector of Eyam William Mompesson came from Biddick. Mompesson persuaded his parishioners to stay in Eyam rather than flee and carry the plague with them. Most of them died as a result.

Until 1750 the dominant local family were the Hiltons. Then they sold their estate in Usworth. Part of it was bought by William Peareth of Newcastle, the current head of a family of Newcastle merchants who dated back to the 16th Century. His new estate included the hall (ie. Usworth House) which was described by the historian Surtees as:

'A handsome stone edifice, of regular architecture, in an open commanding situation with an extensive prospect to the South and East. The mansion is sheltered by a fine grove in the North and West and the grounds are scattered over with lofty, flourishing evergreens, yew, cypress and Lusitanian laurel'.

A VE Day Street Party
The event was at Railway Terrace. In the background is Usworth Colliery.

Usworth Workingmen's Club
The large building on the left was the Usworth Workingmen's Club (the Top Club). It later moved to Sulgrave. Leading off in the distance on the right is a long brick built terrace. To the extreme right foreground is a block of stone built shops and houses including the Stile Inn.

Views at USWORTH 1234

Views of Usworth
This includes three views of Usworth Army Training Camp. It is what is known as a multi-view card. Each of the views will have been available in its own right as an individual card. It is claimed, incidentally, that the family of Ned Kelly the famous Australian bushranger came from Usworth.

Best wishes from Usworth Camp
An R. Johnston and Son (Gateshead) card. It is written in pencil. It is not a standard divided card. The message reads: 'Dear Mother, Father and Sister. Hope you are quite well. We are having nice weather. I went on a march to Sunderland today. We got to camp at 8.30 last night. You could see the sea at Sunderland as we went by. It looked lovely with the ships on. There is about a mile of sands. And all trenches and barbed wire along the coast and a cruiser patrolling along all day. Love Harry. XXX'

R. Johnston & Son, Gateshead.

BEST WISHES from
USWORTH CAMP.

61

Peeps of Washington

The next two cards are general 'sampler' views of the Washington area but they do nicely to conclude these sections on village scenes.

This is an R. Johnston and Sons, Monarch Series postcard. There is no indication of date.

A multi-view of Washington

Another Monarch Series postcard. The date may be 1903. The card is addressed to Miss Gillatt, Boyne Hill House, Chapelthorpe, Nr. Wakefield, Yorkshire. It was sent from The Oval, Washington.

GOING SHOPPING

You'll be staggered by the prices. Naturally the Co-operative Societies figure largely in this section. At the Beamish North of England Open Air Museum you can actually revisit a Co-op of the pre-1914 era. The 'divvi' was an important factor in a family income. In this section watch out for the curious visitor to Walter Willson's, an Eamonn de Valera look-alike and a twisted shop!

Birtley Co-op, Fatfield Branch
The omnipresent Pelaw Boot Polish advert is very prominent. There is also a reference to an 'Exhibition' in the window. That could be an exhibition associated with the 50th Anniversary of the Society which was advertised in the Co-op booklet of 1911. The Birtley Society started off in 1861 in rented property in Mount Pleasant as grocery and provision dealers. A branch was opened in Washington on the corner of Spout Lane in January 1874. The Fatfield branch was opened in 1909. The Society was rightfully celebrating its anniversary. When it started in 1861 it had 148 members, capital of £265, a profit of £77 and a first dividend of 2 shillings. By 1910 there were 4,580 members, a capital of £89,206, profits of £40,175 and a dividend of 3s 7½d.

Chester-le-Street Co-op, Fatfield Branch
Addressed to Mrs Jas. Stout, Low Eighton, Low Fell, Nr. Gateshead. The
message reads: 'Dear T. and F. will come on Saturday if weather permits.
Looked for you coming this week. Hope you got home safe on Sunday. Love
from Aggie.'

Confusingly Fatfield had two Co-ops of different societies and both opened in
1909. The Chester-le-Street Society was established in 1862 by a group of
moulders and engineers from Murray's Old Engine Works. It was intended to
counteract the high prices of shopkeepers and was in reaction against a
particular instance of parsimony. The Chester-le-Street Jubilee History and
Handbook of 1912 reports: 'to make things still worse, the little customary gift
of a penny candle on a quarter of a pound of fourpenny currants at Christmas
time was decided by themselves to be discontinued.' The society started with
eight members and capital of £3 10s in a back room. The first wholesale
purchases were seven pounds of tea, a few stones of sugar, a box of blacking
and a cask of soda. By 1911 membership was 5,090, the share capital was
£143,611 and profits were £58,442. The first store was built at Chester-le-Street
in 1869 and caused a brief crisis of confidence because it was believed that the
society had overstretched itself!

As the success of the Society grew more and more branches were opened. This
Fatfield one was opened in June 1909. It still stands by the river side between
the Havelock Arms and The Biddick. Since the 1980s it has been a club/bar
called, imaginatively, the Inn Between. There is also the exotically named
Fiume Pizzeria. It is still very much the Fatfield Co-op inside though!

The Wholesale Cash Grocery Co.
The window adverts include one for marmalade. The sign above the shop name says 'Importers of Danish and Irish Produce'. Jack Lowther of Birtley, the owner of Lowther's Garages, also owned a chain of five shops until the 1930s. This was one of them in Washington.

Birtley Co-op, Washington Branch
This is the Spout Lane branch which was opened in 1874 standing at the junction of Front Street, Spout Lane and Victoria Road. This was a good site because Spout Lane was the main connecting road between New Washington and Washington Village. It was so successful that it was considerably  extended in 1892. The Co-op had millinery, tailoring, butchers, grocers, crockery, hardware and boot and shoe departments. The Co-op had its own building department as well. It began to invest spare capital in the erection of cottage property in 1893 when work started on some cottages for artisans. This picture dates from 1911 but there is little to date it. Nowadays it is sub-divided into a number of smaller retail units.

CO-OPERATIVE STORES, USWORTH. (757)

Birtley Co-op, Washington Branch
This is actually the Washington Branch of the Birtley Society again, albeit a different angle. The card is addressed to Miss Elsie Walker, 10 Lower Kensington Lane, London. It could be 1913. The message reads: 'My dear Snooks. I have not forgotten you. I was glad to get your letter but there wasn't much in it. When are you going to send me one of your nice ones. Best love. Ethel.' There is a sale in progress. Note the horse droppings in the middle of the street – a common sight in these times!

Birtley Co-op, Washington Branch staff, 1911
There are caps in the left window and blouses in the right. The two boys to the left (one looking suspiciously like Eamonn de Valera!) are well dressed and warmly clad in scarf and gaiters and have watch fobs.

Birtley Co-op, Washington Branch horse and milk float
Here the Co-op horse and milk float have been prepared for the annual horse parade. The man in the straw hat was Andrew Dunkeld, the dairy manager. He passed on his trade to his son Andrew who set up as a milkman independently.

Birtley Co-op, Washington Branch butchery department staff
This was taken in 1912. Of the butchers J.S.Hylton ex-headteacher of High Usworth School recalled: 'Killing day at the store butchers shop brought out early morning shoppers to get the liver and we boys loved to get a pig's bladder to play with.' Simple pleasures!

Co-operative Productions:
Shilling Parcels
There is no indication as to what the
CWS Pelaw Productions parcels
contained but you can bet that there
will have been a tin or two of Pelaw
Metal Polish pushed in here and
there.

Pelaw Polish
This advert is taken from the Chester-
le-Street Co-operative's *History and
Handbook of the Arrangements in
Connection with the Society's Jubilee*
(1912).

Co=operative Productions.

SHILLING PARCELS

OF

Co-operative Productions

WILL BE

On Sale during the Exhibition.

You should not miss the opportunity of Purchasing
a Parcel. as they are worth more money.

C.W.S. Pelaw Productions
..............a Real Treat...............

Have you tried them? If not,

Purchase a Parcel and test for yourselves.

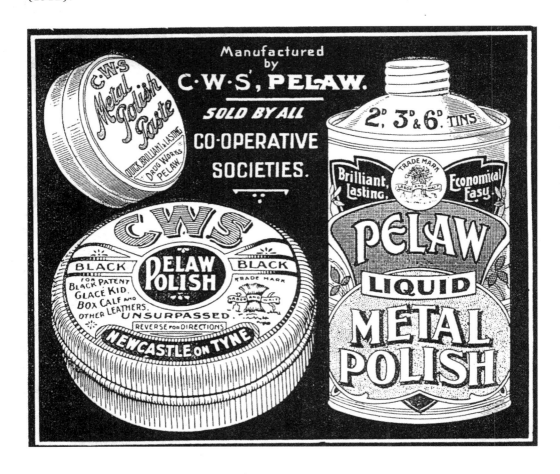

Birtley Co-op, Washington Station Branch
This is another branch of the Birtley co-operative Society in 1911. The
Washington Station Branch was opened in 1901. It was started as a result of
the amalgamation with a small society which was operating in Pattinson Town
in rented property. Land was bought in 1901. The new buildings were
completed in October 1904.

Washington Village Centre
The Cross Keys is to the right. There is an advert for 'Bulwark' on the shop
front.

J.D. Rutherford's
Rutherford was a grocery and provisions merchant. He is standing in the doorway of his shop in Spout Lane. The adverts and product labels are very clear in this photograph. They include Rowntree's Elect Cocoa at $4^1/_2$d a tin and Fray Bentos. HP Sauce is promoted in the right window.

A. Bell's, Butchers
Mr. Bell and a friend are standing at the door. The butcher's shop was originally situated on the west side of Spout Lane just north of the crossroads. This Bell was the ancestor of the Bell family of Columbia which is still in business as caterers.

Pattison's, Grocers
This was known as the 'Busy Little Shop'. It was on Station Road. This view is in 1917. Rowntree's Cocoa and Oxo are very prominent. A sign in the left window tells us 'butter down'. The shop was situated adjacent to the Glebe Schools in Station Road. Later on it became 'Toms Tyres and Batteries'.

J. Anderson's, Drapers
James Anderson's is described glowingly as 'The Smart Clothier Draper'. The men in the street obviously do not frequent Anderson's though. To the right is the shop of W.T. Noble.

Johnson's Stores
This shop was in Wessington Terrace. The eye is captured immediately by the sign '10 Bandmaster Pure Virginia Cash Bonus Cigarettes. 4d'.

Forte's Confectioners and Billiard Saloon
Forte's in Station Terrace (nearly opposite the junction with Edith Avenue) in 1922. In the doorway are Mr Giovanni Forte, his sister Maria and his daughter Mary. An early Ford car stands in front of the premises. In the window, framed by the Fry's Chocolate adverts, can be seen the faces of Messrs Matty Bolam, Tom Nayden and Henry Bannister. Some things are more important than billiards.

Helens, at the bottom of Station Road
The shop, owned by Miss Edith Forster, was popular with Chemical Works' staff and known for its home made cakes.

W.T. Noble's, Drapers and Outfitters
W.T. Noble's was a drapers and outfitters on the north side of Front Street near the junction with Manor Road. There is a line of buses and taxis outside the shop. The enterprising Mr Noble was also in the transport business. This was taken in 1922.

Brady Square
Anderson's Newsagents is to the right. Kensitas cigarettes are advertised. Of course there is the 'News of the World: All Human Life is There'. We're talking pre-Page Three 'Stunnas' here naturally.

Granny Witts Shop
This is the famous 'Granny Witts' shop in Wellbank Road. Looking down from the bank the roof looked distorted. It is claimed to be because when the builders pegged out the site Mrs Witt came during the night and moved a peg to get a larger house for her money. The result was that when the roof was put on it was twisted. Wellbank is so-called because there was a well just across the road from the chapel.

MINING AND OTHER INDUSTRIES

Originally the area was agricultural and rural. However there were pits on Washington Moor as long ago as 1356. The great surge in mining activity in this region began in the later 18th Century. The concept of an 'Industrial Revolution' in the later 18th Century is unfashionable but judging from output in the northern coalfield and coal exports from the Wear it was a very real phenomenon in the mining and coal export industries. The industry spawned its own very distinctive communities because the employers wanted their labour supply to be very close so they provided housing, schools and chapels and other facilities. Of course the other great industry in this area, all but obliterated from view and memory now, was the internationally significant chemical industry.

A mining deputy

There is no indication as to who this is or where the photograph was taken. Nevertheless he is obviously a pit deputy so he is a good guide to accompany us around a tour of the mining industry at Washington.

Chatershaugh Pit, Harraton Colliery
Looking south west to the colliery in the distance along the tracks of a branch of the Harraton waggonway. The large building in the centre right is Ruddock's Copperas House. The low stone buildings to the left of the photograph (and in front of the colliery) housed the original Ferry Boat Inn. The date will be about 1900.

Chatershaugh Pit, Harraton Colliery
Here can be seen part of Fatfield Primitive Methodist Church, the south end of the East side of Castle Street at the right and the Chatershaugh shaft of Harraton Colliery in the background. This will be in the 1960s.

Cotia Pit, Harraton Colliery

The pit was closed down on the 29th May, 1965. Salvage work underground was finished by 1966. The demolition of the surface buildings was carried out in August 1966.

Harraton is on the outskirts of New Washington. Its name is derived from the ancient manor of Havertune which was originally in the ownership of the Bishops of Durham but was passed from Ranulf Flambard to his brother in 1277 and thence to the Darcys and Hedworths.

Shafts were sunk on the Biddick estate in the earl 17th Century. Ownership was interrupted by the Civil War. In 1714 though the estate was reunited under Lambton ownership. Until 1642 the owner was Sir John Hedworth. On his death in that troubled year the estate passed to his son John who was a Royalist and who lost control of the colliery and a large part of his estate to parliamentary officers 'on the make'. John was succeeded by his son John, confusingly, in 1655. He managed partly to retrieve the family fortunes. Then when he died in 1688 he left two heiresses – Dorothy (the eldest) was married to Ralph Lambton while the youngest married William Williamson of Whitburn Hall. In 1714 a marriage between the two families brought most of the estate back together. It remained in the hands of the Lambtons until 1896. Before nationalisation Harraton was one of 22 collieries under Lambton and Joicey ownership.

The real name of this pit was Nova Scotia Pit. That may be because of the large number of Scots who worked here – refugees from even harsher conditions in Fife. It may be though that the name reflects some contemporary imperial feat (as with places like Quebec, Philadelphia, or Bunker Hill).

Rickleton Village stands on the site of the colliery today. The curious and famous Colliers Rant originated from this area. The colliery was connected to the Wear Staithes at Chartershaugh by a $1^1/_2$ mile wooden railway. Originally there were a dozen pits but in modern times there were only two main shafts, the Big Shaft and the Billy Shaft.

Harraton was noted for innovation in mining. In 1732 Fatfield Colliery saw the first attempt at artificial ventilation using fire lamps and furnaces. In 1756 North Biddick Colliery was the first to use a furnace on the surface at the bottom of a tall chimney instead of at the bottom of a shaft. In 1763 it was at Fatfield Colliery that steel mill lighting made its appearance. That predominated until the safety lamp made its appearance. There is even a claim that the Davy Lamp was first used at the Lambton Colliery.

Cotia Pit, Harraton Colliery

Of course one of the most famous owners was John George Lambton in whose honour Penshaw Monument was built. An unbelievably wealthy man by the standards of the time he was known as 'King Jog' because he once remarked cheerily that he could 'jog along on £40,000 a year.'

Locomotive No. 2308

This was LC 21 0-4-0 No. 2308. It was used at Lambton and Scotia Collieries. It was built in 1876 by Robert Stephenson and Co., South Street, Newcastle. It went to NCB No. 2 area in 1947 and its route was extended to Forth Banks. It was scrapped in 1954. The man with the duster is Tom Carr.

F Pit, Washington Colliery
This is a view of F Pit and the waste heap.

Fordyce describes the Washington Colliery and its community in 1857 in these words:

'Washington Colliery, situated a little to the west of the main township, is an extensive concern, at present worked by Messrs Bell and Partners. The main coal is at a depth of 75 fathoms, and the Maudlin, Low Main and Hutton Seams successively 10 fathoms below each other, making a total depth of 105 fathoms. Washington Row is a hamlet inhabited by persons employed in the adjoining coal works and contains a Wesleyan Methodist Chapel.'

Washington Colliery

F Pit's origins are as far back as 1775 when the land was leased to William Russell and Partners. A series of pits were sunk. They became New Washington Colliery. The pits were lettered from A to I. F was sunk in 1777. That was the year before the first coals were shipped from the colliery by waggonway to Sunderland. F Pit was closed from 1796-1820 because it filled with water following an explosion. It was reopened in 1820 and then deepened in 1856. It became the main coal outlet for the colliery. It was remodelled in 1903 for the third time. In 1947 it was nationalised and became part of the No. 1 Area of the North Eastern Division. It was deepened in the 1950s. By the 1960s F Pit produced 486,000 tons of saleable coal a year and employed 1500 men. It was closed on the 21st June 1968 when it was the oldest working pit in the country. The winding house and pit-head gear were preserved though and it was reopened as a museum in 1976 by the Washington Development Corporation. In 1984 responsibility for it passed to the Tyne and Wear Museums Service.

F Pit and Granary Row

Single Row with the F Pit in the background
At one time another Row of houses lay behind these known as Quarry Row.

F Pit, Washington Colliery

The colliery waste heap rose to a height of 61 metres (or 200 feet) and dominated the sky-line of the old town before its removal after the closure of the pit. Originally F Pit will have had a water-wheel powered winding engine with a Newcomen steam pumping engine. That raised the coal in large hazel baskets or corves attached to hemp ropes. These had a disconcerting tendency to spin or collide with the wall or each other. The ropes tended to snap as well. This was reduced by the introduction of conductors up the sides of the shaft, the use of flat ropes and then wire ropes from the 1830s. By the 1830s steam winding was prevalent and the corves were replaced by a cage. The essentials of this pithead apparatus date to 1903 when F Pit was remodelled.

J.S.Hylton recalled:
'Before electricity was supplied the fan of the upcast shaft at Washington was worked by steam and there was always a huge supply of hot water in iron tanks just outside the engine house. As boys we had to take buckets up there and bring back hot water for washing days or for personal baths in the tin bath in front of the kitchen fire.'

F Pit Putters
The date is 1910. Here can be seen John George Nicholson on the left and Henry Smith on the right. Putters supplied the face workers with empty tubs and removed full tubs to a flat. They also did additional tasks such as taking in pit props, bricks, rails etc. This work was either done by hand or with the aid of a pony.

F Pit Colliery Manager's House
This is a front view of Hill House when Mr Thomas Burn was the manager. It still stands in Village Lane.

There are two amazing men associated with Washington Colliery – the pitman millionaire George Elliott and the mathematics prodigy James Hann. Elliott worked at Washington Colliery as a pitman. He was born in 1815 at Penshaw the son of a miner. He left school at the age of nine and went to work. However he went to night school and rose to become the colliery manager. Then he became owner of Oxclose, Biddick and Penshaw Pits and of pits in South Wales. He was also part owner, with Frederick Newall, of a wire rope factory which made the first submarine cable laid from England to America. He was involved in persuading Disraeli to buy shares in the Suez Canal – an action which was to have major effects on the foreign and imperial policies of Britain. He became an MP in 1868 and a baronet in 1874. He died in 1893 and is buried in Houghton le Spring.

Elliott will have been at the colliery at the same time as James Hann who looked after the pit engines. He taught himself to read and write. In 1835 he won the 'All England Prize for Mathematics'. He was given a post at the Greenwich Observatory and became a master at Kings College London. He wrote a number of books and treatises on steam engines, bridges and machinery. He died in 1856.

Washington Colliery F.C.
The date is 1917-18

Victoria Bridge, Fatfield.

North Biddick Colliery
North Biddick Colliery had the local dialect name of 'Butney' which was a
corruption of Botany Bay. Workers from the Penshaw area crossed the river by
means of a ferry boat near Victoria Bridge which was managed by an overhead
cable and a wheel. In 1900 the colliery employed about 350 men and boys. It
was closed in the 1930s when it became uneconomic. It had a vast spoil heap
which was landscaped by Washington New Town.

North Biddick Colliery
This is a longer perspective view of the colliery. A mixed freight train is crossing the bridge.

Glebe Pit, Washington
The offices are to the right. The pit canteen does not seem to have been built when this photograph was taken. It was famous for its pies and peas. The Glebe was the first shaft in Britain to be sunk using the freezing process, and the last to be sunk at Washington. The name originates incidentally from the fact that the colliery was built on land given to support the priest in the Middle Ages. Work on it began in 1901. There were two shafts, No. 1(876 feet deep) and No. 2 (800 feet deep). The first coal was drawn in 1905.

Fancy Dress Football
This event was arranged to raise funds for the support of the 1921 strike at the Glebe Colliery.

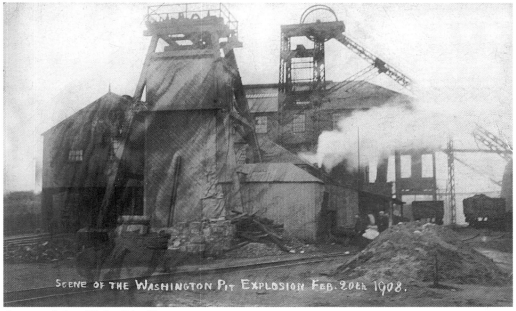

SCENE OF THE WASHINGTON PIT EXPLOSION FEB. 20th 1908.

Scene of the Glebe Pit disaster
The explosion occurred on the 20th February, 1908. In the course of the resultant fire the rescuers were driven back six times. Fourteen pitmen were killed. Of course tragedies like this one recurred frequently through the history of mining in Washington. Indeed in the north west corner of Washington parish churchyard are buried the bodies of the miners lost at Oxclose on 29th November 1805, and they included the three young Knott brothers, William (18), Thomas (15) and Edward (12).

Glebe Pit Disaster, Funeral Scenes

There were 22,000 people present in the Washington Station area for the funeral of Messrs Wake (42), Cowan (44) and Madden (37). There was a cortege of about a mile in length. The contemporary press report was as follows:

'Sad as were the scenes of Saturday when the bodies of the dead miners were taken to their homes for a temporary halt prior to their last earthly journey, the scenes of Sunday, when three of the deceased men were interred in the little cemetery at Old Washington, eclipsed anything ever witnessed in the district.

Hundreds of people went to Washington from all over the county of Durham and Northumberland and owing to the lack of trains the journey was made in all manner of vehicles from the more costly motor car to the humble country wagonette. The vast majority of the visitors, of course, were miners who had gone to the village to pay a final tribute of respect to their comrades who had lost their lives in the sunless caverns of the mine.'

Glebe Pit Disaster Postcard Offer
Obviously not going too well or reduced as the impulse of immediacy lessened the sales. Of course we might not produce and sell postcards in this way today but that is simply because we have much more immediate ways of gaining graphic access to catastrophic scenes and displays of grief.

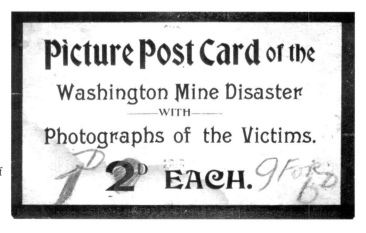

The various portraits are labelled: WALTER HENRY MULLEN, HARRY OSWALD, THOMAS APPLEGARTH, ROBERT COWAN, JOHN AMBROSE MADGWICK, JAMES WARE, JOHN DIXON, ALFRED WOOD, THOMAS McNALLY, JOHN CLARK, EDWARD ASHMAN, THOMAS ERRINGTON, WILLIAM GLENDINNING, CHARLES CHIVERS, DAMAGED UP-CAST SHAFT, GENERAL VIEW OF COLLIERY.

DURHAM MINE DISASTER.
FIRE DAMP EXPLOSION AT THE GLEBE COLLIERY, WASHINGTON.
14 MINERS CRUSHED AND BURNT TO DEATH, AND ONE SERIOUSLY INJURED. THURSDAY, FEBRUARY 20TH, 1908.
PUBLISHED BY W. GOTHARD, 6, ELDON STREET, BARNSLEY. WHOLESALE : W. H. SMITH & SONS, FORTH PLACE, NEWCASTLE-ON-TYNE

Glebe Pit Disaster
The date of the postcard is the 7th March, 1908. It is addressed to Miss Wood, Commercial Street, Willington, County Durham.

The families of Strikers at Fatfield
There is a police escort. There are a number of wives and children. One of the women is beating a drum. This could be a protest against the employment of strike-breakers, or they could be emphasising their support for the strikers. This seems a good humoured occasion. The location is probably Bonemill Lane. The raised bank can be seen in the background, and above that is the embankment of the Harraton Waggonway.

The Old Glebe Banner
This group is assembled in Emmerson Terrace. It is not clear whether a procession has taken place or is about to take place.

Miners' Welfare Hall, Washington
This is in Concord today. One of the houses is marked with a cross but there is no indication as to why. This was a postcard though so someone has probably marked it in the way that you might indicate a hotel in Majorca.

Washington Colliery Prize Band, 1956
This was one of the leading brass bands of the day. The pride in its
achievements is very easy to see here.

Washington Colliery Band
The band is marching down Spout Lane towards the Miners' Welfare Hall. The
photographer has caught the atmosphere of the occasion splendidly.

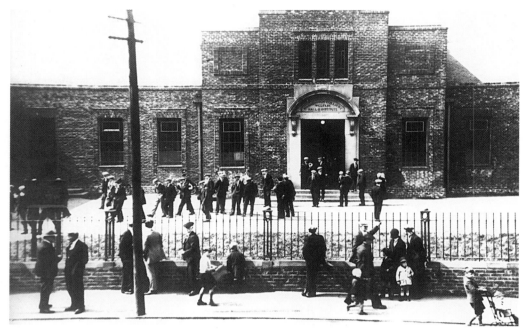

Miners' Welfare Hall, Washington
The Hall was opened in 1931. The Miners' Hall stood in Spout Lane. It was owned by the colliery. The building is now the New London Inn and an Indian Restaurant. There is a boy with a push-chair disappearing off the picture at the bottom right corner. The Miners' Welfare Hall had a billiards hall and other recreation facilities. It was used for dances and for meetings of all sorts. In fact it looks as if a meeting has just ended.

Usworth Colliery
Looking north west to the pithead gear, winding house and surrounding buildings. The colliery was sunk in 1845. The original owners were Messrs Jonassohn and Elliott. Later it was taken over by Messrs John Bowes and Partners Ltd. It employed about 750 men and boys in the 1890s. It was closed in 1974.

Miners collecting coal from Usworth Colliery waste heap
This was during the 1921 strike. The comedian Bobby Thompson recalled
enhancing his income in the same way in 1931. His dole then was 7s 6d a
week. He scoured the coal heaps with other miners and sold bags of coal at 6d
a bag.

Usworth Colliery miners and children
This is a 1928 photograph. Included are: Tom Varty, Jim Liddle, Ike Simpson,
George Varty, Dennis Kelly, J. Kenyon, Joe Kenyon, Oliver Curry, Billy Felton,
Barty Ward, Jonty Simpson, Tom Merrigan, Jack Kirtley, George Curry, Harry
Hann, 'Gunner' Golden, Addy Greenwell, Tom Pringle, Syd Kirtley, Jack
Pringle, Leo Liddle, Billy Liddle, John Simpson, Jim Simpson, Joseph Simpson,
Jim Davidson. Notice the frequent repetition of family names.

Usworth Colliery, Durham Miners' Gala Day
The date is 1950. The procession with the colliery band and second banner is crossing the Elvet Bridge on the way to the race course.

A Special Train for the Durham Miners' Gala
This is at Washington Station in 1958. A train enters the station with a special from Usworth to the Durham Miners Gala.

Miners' Hall and Institute, Usworth Colliery
The date on the plaque is 1891 to save you straining your eyes. There are also
a couple of faces at the lower second left window. The Miners' Hall and
Institute was built in 1891 at a cost of £1800. It contained a lecture theatre
with seats for 650 people, reading rooms, billiards rooms and a committee
room and caretaker's quarters.

Usworth Colliery Welfare Pavilion
This is a real bowling action shot! It's about as much action as you'll get
anyhow.

The waste heap of Newall's Chemical Works
The 'white heap' was a hundred years old when this was taken. It towers over the Barmston Ferry Houses and Washington Staithes. This historic photograph was taken before work started on reclamation at Barmston Ferry, and will have been taken somewhere between 1958 and 1970.

Newall's Chemical Works
This is the chemical works in all its grim glory. In the distance to the right you can also see the waste heap of F Pit.

Chemical Works

The Chemical Works were started at Washington Station in 1837 by Hugh Lee Pattinson after whom the village of Pattinson Town is known. A chemist by trade he came from Alston and took over what had been a bleaching mill. He patented processes for separating silver from lead, for manufacturing white lead and then for extracting magnesia from limestone. The main product of the Washington Chemical Company established in 1842 was lead carbonate for paintmaking but it branched out into a range of chemicals. Pattinson died in 1858 but his business was carried on by his four sons-in-law. From 1873 Frederick Sterling Newall was senior manager of the Chemical Company and that was when the production of magnesia chemicals was vastly increased and Newall's became the largest producer in the world. From 1851 Newall was also producing telegraphic cable and laid the first successful cables from Dover to Calais. The firm also produced Cork Insulation, Insulating Bricks and Carbonic Acid Gas.

The need for casks for washing soda meant that a lot of coopers were employed as well. The first cooper from 1846 was a Mr J. Burden who walked from South Shields and back each day. He died in 1911 only two years after receiving a gold watch and illuminated address.

Blast Row in the shadow of the Chemical Works

A visit to a licensee in the USA had revealed to Newall the idea of combining magnesium carbonate and short fibre chrysotile asbestos to produce a very malleable insulation material which was ideal for pipes and boilers. Manufacture began at Washington in 1893. It was vastly stimulated by the First World War. Then in 1920 Newall's was one of four firms to amalgamate to form Turner and Newall Ltd. In 1925 this firm purchased a majority shareholding in Ferodo Ltd. which specialised in clutch and brake linings.

The activities of Pattinson and his sons-in-law were so extensive and innovative that it is surprising that they have not been studied and recorded in more depth.

Using both tractor and horse and cart at High Washington
These farm scenes may be on High Washington Farm near F Pit.

Using a harvester at High Washington
Certainly that is the F Pit waste heap far off in the background.

CHURCH AND CHAPEL

All of the main religious denominations have a strong presence in Washington's past and present. However it was protestant non-conformism, and especially Methodism, which played a very major role in the development of the communities. That was not simply a question of religion. It was also because the chapel was a focal centre for all sorts of other related community activities. Also involvement in chapel management and preaching was a training ground for unionists and miners leaders. In this section we encounter the church with the wrong name, catch the scent of a pickled parson and enjoy cocoa at a Mission.

WESLEYAN CHAPEL, WASHINGTON

Wesleyan Chapel, Washington
The card is dated 20th December, 1912. It is addressed to the Rev and Mrs Finnegan, Wesley House, Lime Tree Avenue, Retford, Notts. The message reads: 'The Manse, Washington Village, Co. Durham. The seasons greetings and every good wish from R. and D. Browell'.

Chatershaugh Wesleyan Chapel

The chapel is no longer there. That is sad because this was a very historic building. It was a Wesleyan chapel. Such chapels played a very vital part in their community. There would be something on every night. These included the meetings of the Brotherhood and the Sisterhood, the youth groups like the Boy Scouts and the Girl Guides and the Junior Endeavour and Senior Endeavour, the chapel choir (probably practicing the Messiah) and the Sunday School. There was little else to do that cost nothing. One of the highlights of the year would be the Sunday School trip which usually went to exotic places like South Shields, Finchale Abbey or Roker. Other entertainments would include mock baptisms and weddings.

This chapel was built in 1784. The group was known until 1796 as the Biddick or North Biddick Society. It was known as the Chatershaugh Society only from 1796. The site of the chapel was eventually taken over by the Colliery and it was demolished to make way for a pumping plant.

Wesley certainly visited South Biddick in 1747 because he records the visit in his Journal:

'Tuesday, 22nd March. I went to South Biddick, a village of collieries seven miles south east of Newcastle. The spot where I stood was just at the bottom of a semi-circular hill, on the rising sides of which many hundreds stood; but far more in the plain beneath. I cried to them in the words of the prophet 'O ye dry bones, hear the Word of the Lord!' Deep attention sat on every face; so that here also I believed it would be well to preach weekly.'

Wesley's definition of his typical early converts was 'low, insignificant people! poor almost to a man'.

Trinity Church,
Washington Village
It is said that there was
originally a Saxon church
on the site which dated back
to the 10th Century. The
care of the parish was in the
hands of the Benedictine
monks of Thorney Abbey to
whom it was granted in 973
AD by King Edgar. The rota
of known Rectors begins in
1196 AD with a John. The
original church was in a
very delapidated state by the
1830s. It was demolished in
April 1832. Holy Trinity
(1831-33) was built by John

and Benjamin Green of Newcastle. It cost £1096 of which the Rector Henry
Perceval (1826-27) contributed £468. It was built in the Early English style.
The west door arch and the 12th Century font are all that remains of the
medieval church. The remodelled church was not well regarded because of its
plainness and flattened roof. In fact it was known as 'the barn' by its critics!
Partly in response to these criticisms the nave was lengthened, transepts added
and roof raised in 1882-83. In 1902 the chancel was extended. A bell tower
was added in 1962.

Originally the parish of Washington included Usworth and North Biddick as
well as Washington and Barmston. Then in 1832 Usworth was made a separate
ecclesiastical parish. In 1881 North Biddick was transferred to Harraton.

Trinity Church, Washington Village

The Trinity Church, Washington Village
There are better views of the church elsewhere in this book. What is interesting about this card is the message. It was addressed to a Miss Isa Cooke, Station Road, Backworth, Newcastle-upon-Tyne but the sender's name is not recorded. The date seems to be 1906. It reads simply:

> 'I know maiden, oh so fair,
> Take care, beware.
> Trust her not, she's fooling thee,
> Trust her not she's fooling thee!'

The Rectory, Washington
Washington Rectory had a chequered history. It was built in 1719-27 by Rector Richard Stonehewer then enlarged in 1868 by Rector J. Shadwell. It was burnt down in 1926 and rebuilt. It was bought by the District Council in 1937. It was burnt down again in 1949 and rebuilt as the offices of the Washington District Council but modelled on the old Rectory. Prior to 1937 the UDC offices were in Front Street.

Canon Cyril Lomax outside the Rectory

This impressive figure was Canon Cyril Lomax, the 56th Rector of Washington (there was another, apparently unrelated, Lomax in the post just before him). He took up the Living in 1899. He had been educated at Keble College, Oxford then been Curate at Weaste in Lancashire (1895-97) and Curate at Washington for two years (1897-99). He was a chaplain to the territorial forces and served in the First World War as Senior Chaplain to the 63rd Division, with the 151st Infantry Brigade in France and then with the Duke of Cornwalls Light Infantry and East Yorkshires in troubled post-war Ireland. He was recalled by Mr J.S. Hylton ex-headteacher of High Usworth School: 'The Rev Mr Lomax rode around his parish on horseback like a country squire, and if we could only catch him dismounting to visit a parishioner we held the horse rein and were rewarded with a penny. Mr Lomax followed the hounds and when he went on his annual holiday he sent his horse for a holiday too.'

Pickled Parson

This is an appropriate point to dispose of the famous 'pickled parson'. It is claimed that in 1747 the wife of the Rector, John Gamage, preserved his body in salt in a chest for several days until Christmas Day (as you do!) when the local farmers were due to pay their tithe. The tithe having been paid she then laid out her husband's body in bed and reported his death. In fact the story is more properly associated with Sedgfield because John Gamage left Washington to go there in 1728. You do wonder why the farmers weren't more observant. Not content with that escapade John Gamage also haunted the Sedgefield Rectory until it was destroyed by fire in 1792.

Holy Trinity, Usworth
It was built in 1831-32 by the Rev Henry Perceval. He was Rector of Charlton in Kent, then Vicar of Hoathley in Sussex (1825-26) then Rector at Washington in 1826-37. He moved on to become Rector of Elmley-Lovett in Worcester in 1837-83. He died in April 1885. He was actually the son of the Prime Minister

Spencer Perceval who was assassinated by deranged Bellingham in 1812 in St Stephen's Hall, Westminster.

The church was opened in April 1832. It was dedicated to The Holy Trinity. It was described then as 'a neat structure of stone', and so it appears here. It was designed by Greens of Newcastle in the Early Pointed Gothic style. In fact this new building and the rebuilding of Washington Church were both part of the Grand Plan of Perceval and the Anglican establishment to try and match the success of the Methodists by providing more spaces. Despite that Methodism continued to thrive because of the opening of new collieries, distance from the Anglican centres and the influx of miners from the staunchly Wesleyan and Primitive Methodist Weardale area.

Usworth Colliery Chapel, Edith Avenue
The chapel is now used as a community centre. The houses to the left are still there but Edith Avenue has gone.

Catholic Church, Washington. 3325

The Catholic Church, Washington

This is the Our Blessed Lady Immaculate Church in Village Lane. It was built
in 1877-78 by A.M. Dunn. The presbytery is to the right. The Catholic
population was fairly small until the big Irish influx from the 1830s and 1840s.
In 1863 a school and Mass Centre were set up in Village Lane in Washington
by Father Joseph Brown of Houghton who commuted by horse via Fatfield
ferry. Then in August 1877 the *Newcastle Chronicle* recorded:

'The memorial stone of a new Catholic Church at Washington was laid by the
Bishop of Hexham and Newcastle yesterday, in the presence of a very large
assembly of spectators. The memorial stone which forms the foundation of the
South pier was prepared in the usual manner, and a sealed bottle containing
several documents was placed in the cavity of the stone.'

It cost £4000 and was designed by Messrs Dunn and Hanson of Eldon Square.
The land was provided by Mr Newall.

Oddly enough the church was mis-named. It was intended by the priest Father
Cambours that it should be dedicated to The Immaculate Conception but in
error he allowed it to enter the official Calender under the name of the Mass
Centre ie. St Joseph's. Not until 1933 was it officially consecrated as the
Church of Our Blessed Lady Immaculate.

Village Lane Wesleyan Chapel, Washington
This was the Village Lane Chapel, dismissed by 'Prims' as 'All kid-gloves and lavender' because the Wesleyans were rather more 'up-market'. Miners were more likely to be Primitive Methodists. The plaque on the wall says 1877. The chapel was closed and amalgamated with the Joseph Cook Memorial Chapel in the 1970s.

Station Road Primitive Methodist Sunday School
This is a 1920s photograph of a Sunday School group from Station Road Primitive Methodist Chapel with 'The Childrens Tribute'. There are 34 pretty girls and four rather disconsolate boys. Most of the girls have floral headbands on. The poor boys are having to hold up the sign 'The Childrens Tribute'. How embarrassing for them!

Station Road Primitive Methodist Chapel
This group is assembled to have a photograph taken on the day of the opening
of the 'tin hut' which was used for all sorts of functions. This scene is in 1950.
There were Primitive Methodist chapels in Little Usworth, Washington Staithes
(1851), Usworth Colliery (1863), Harraton Colliery (1875) and in Brady
Square, Washington Station. This latter was intended to target the chemical
works and rope and cable factory.

*Station Road
Chapel Women's
Concert Party*
A splendid set of
gypsies these
ladies make as
well! Primitive
Methodism
was very strong
in colliery
districts and
could rely on the
enthusiasm of its
congregation to
create very active
communities.
In 1909 W.M.
Patterson, the

great historian of Primitive Methodism, wrote: 'The opening of a new Colliery
at Washington Station quickly attracted energetic 'prims' to it, and a society
was soon established. Its growth was extraordinarily rapid, and the erection of
a building for worship was speedily accomplished. With half a dozen local
preachers and sixty members in 1907, in a mining place the best is possible.
Unhappily the toll of death in the mine claimed one of its useful officials,
Robert Cowen, in the explosion of February 20th 1908 (Glebe Pit).'

Cook Memorial Wesleyan Church, North Biddick circa 1904

This chapel was built in 1900 sponsored by Joseph Cook who was the owner of the Iron Foundry. Methodism was reintroduced to Biddick in 1852. Services were held in the kitchen of North Biddick Hall. Then in May 1858 a room in a cottage in Biddick Row was obtained. Then on the 18th June, 1860 the foundation stone of the chapel at North Biddick

was laid by Lowthian Bell. The driving force of methodism in North Biddick though was Joseph Cook. Later on the old chapel was converted to cottages and a new one was built in 1900 at Brady Square at the south end of Albert Place. The Cook family subscribed money to that as well. That chapel was demolished in 1977. The congregation joined the Glebe Chapel. Several street names in the area still commemorate the Cook connection eg. Harold Street, Albert Place.

St Cuthbert's Mission, Station Road circa 1909

In the picture is St Cuthbert's Mission (Anglican) which was taken over in later years (along with the next two houses) by Mr Tom Bell and converted for storage use by his catering firm. There is also Walter Willson's which is now part of the Celtic Club. To the left of that is Moore's the grocers shop. Most of these houses have now gone. Even the delivery horse is staring at the camera!

St George's Church and Fatfield School
There is St George's Church in the background. The school, on the right, is
Fatfield Primary School. This is Bonemill Lane. The raised bank and
embankment are very clear here. Wagons came down the lane here to
Chatershaugh from Harraton Colliery. This scene is now radically changed
because the dual carriageway cuts through it and obscures the church from
this angle. The school was closed in July 1998 and then demolished.

Church Bank, Fatfield
Probably in the 1950s. There are Swiss cottages to the left. They are still there.
One of them is used as a doctor's surgery. St George's Church, Fatfield is an
Anglican church. The parish of Fatfield was formed in 1875. The church was
built in 1879.

St George's Church
The church cost £5000 to build. The cost was met by the Earl of Durham. It
was designed by Messrs Walter Scott and Son of Sunderland. It is made of red
brick dressed with stone. The oak choir stalls and brass lectern are actually
from Bishopwearmouth Church from whence they were brought when it was
undergoing some rebuilding in 1935. It is quite an attractive church with its
striking slender spiral belfry, and is very visible.

St Cuthbert's Mission Hall Soup Kitchen 1914-18
Frys Pure Breakfast Cocoa and baskets of loaves of bread. These are helpers at
the Mission who ran the soup kitchen between 1914-18. Holding the cocoa box
is Mr Sandy. Brady Square is in the left background, and Rutter's Shop to the
extreme left.

The Rev W.S. Reeman,
Vicar of Fatfield

The Rev W.S. Reeman was the Vicar of Fatfield for an amazing 58 years, and a clergyman for 68 years. He died at home in 1935 at the age of 91. He came to Fatfield in 1876. Then there was no church and services were held in the old reading room. The church was built in 1879 by the Earl of Durham. Reeman was described as: 'a champion of modern youth'. He admired their keenness for open-air pastimes. 'To my mind' he once said 'the young people today are as reliable and trustworthy as their parents and grandparents were.' He had conducted 2,200 baptisms, 640 marriages and 1,926 funerals.

Washington United AFC

They were based at the Wesleyan Chapel, Engine Square. They were a team in the Washington District League and Washington Area Miners' Cup. On the plaque it says 'Season 1913-14.' Many football teams, and many of those in the national league, started life based on a church or chapel or some other institution. Often they had the active backing of local employers. This was very much because organised sport was seen as a subtle form of social control. The alternative uses of unorganised leisure time, mostly on Sundays, could too easily be drunkenness and violence.

Mission Church of St Michael and All Angels, Usworth Colliery
This brick structure was erected in 1894 at a cost of £750 and with 200
sittings. It looks newly built. It seems as if work on the drains is still going on.

The Church Army travelling van
The Church Army travelling van at Edith Avenue near St Michael's Church.
These mobile units were part of the Anglican strategy to make greater in-roads
in the colliery areas.

> 'The Wages of Sin is Death
> But the Gift of God is Eternal Life
> Him that Cometh unto me
> I will in no wise cast out!'

A good point at which to end this section.

THE BEST DAYS!

Many of the pictures in this section are of schools or are related to schools. Until 1871 state provision of education was limited to state institutions like the armed services, prisons and workhouses. Provision for elementary schooling was dominated by the various religious denominations because of the preference for voluntaryism and charity. Quite often schools were provided by employers. So in this area for instance there was Usworth Colliery School from 1863 and Washington Colliery School from 1899. Then the Forster Education Act introduced the concept of locally elected School Boards which raised a local rate and provided places in elementary schools to remedy deficiencies in provision. Barmston established a school board in 1875, Usworth in 1875 and Washington as late as 1890.

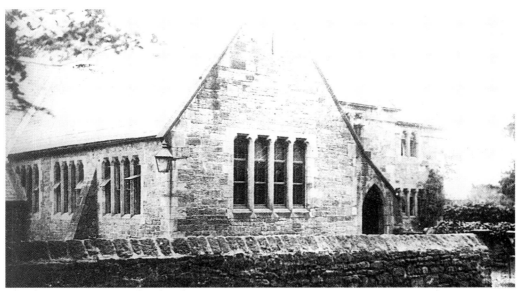

Washington National Schools
The original caption of this postcard simply says 'Washington Schools' but this is the original Church of England school in Washington Village. The Anglican provision consisted mostly of the Susan Peareth charity school at Great Usworth, which was established in 1814, and the National Schools shown here. They were built on the site of Manor House Farm which was demolished in 1856. They were stone buildings with places for 220 mixed and infant children. The usual attendance in the later 19th Century was 180 pupils.

St Joseph's Roman Catholic School
This was the old Catholic School opposite the Catholic church. It burnt down some years ago. The older part of it was actually the original Mass Centre of Father Joseph – the commuting Houghton priest.

St Joseph's Roman Catholic School
This is the Catholic school which was built on the site of the St Joseph's Mass Centre which preceded the Catholic Church of Our Blessed Lady Immaculate. This photograph probably dates from the 1950s.

The former Usworth Colliery School

This was the old Usworth Colliery School which was taken over by Pawson's and converted into a garment factory. Pawson's also took over the Primitive Methodist Chapel which stood in the same grounds. They stood in Edith Avenue, Usworth. The school was created in 1863 by the Usworth Colliery Company. It was made up of mixed and infants departments, and there were 600 places.

Usworth Colliery school used to have a headteacher called John Anderson but known as 'Johnny Pop'. He was there from 1894 to 1928. He is recalled by the former head teacher of High Usworth School, J. S. Hylton:

'If ever there was a Christian gentleman it was John Anderson. He certainly hid his light under a bushel, but his good deeds were legion. Money was put through letter boxes, parcels of groceries were left on doorsteps or delivered to the householders, boots and clothing supplied to needy children and all done surreptitiously' and 'When we were about due for a government inspection he would stand for hours at one of the school windows looking up the road down which the inspectors would come, and shaking with fear all the time'

That latter sounds very much like OFSTED inspection syndrome! Hylton said that when the photographs of groups of children were to be taken the boys were given clean collars while the girls swapped pinafores so that the cleanest and best were most prominent. A new school was opened at High Usworth in 1929. It was destroyed by fire in 1948. Another school was built in 1953, then a junior school was added in 1959.

Usworth Boys Brigade

A hand-written caption says that these are members of the Usworth Colliery School Boys Brigade in 1901. There are 31 boys including the bugler (to the left). The message on the slate seems to say 'Usworth Colliery Board School Boys. Flower Show'. The rifles look very realistic! In fact they are not in the usual uniform of the Boys Brigade although they are clearly in a type of uniform. There were other organisations similar to the Boys Brigade, or perhaps they just haven't got their proper uniforms yet.

The Boys Brigade was founded in 1883 by Sir William Smith of Glasgow during the era of 'muscular christianity' to pursue: 'the advancement of Christ's Kingdom among boys, and the promotion of habits of obedience, reverence, discipline, self-respect and all that tends towards true Christian manliness'. Like a military organisation it was and is made up of companies of boys of 12 to 17 years of age. They were formed in connection with Sunday schools, churches and missions of religious bodies. They wore a distinctive uniform and exercised using a quasi military drill. By 1910 there were about 65,000 members with 6,400 officers.

Washington School Board

The Washington School Board was established in 1890, which was rather late. School Boards were established at Barmston and Usworth in 1875. The Washington School Board proceeded to build the Washington Board School (1893), Washington Biddick School (1892) and Washington Colliery School (1899).

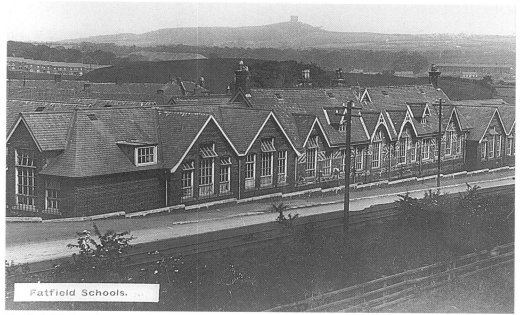

Fatfield School

There is a good view from across the Harraton Waggonway (you can actually see the lines) to Penshaw Monument. East Bridge Street and Beatrice Terrace are clear. The Penshaw Staithes Cottages can just be seen. The North Biddick Colliery pit heaps can be seen behind the school.

Fatfield Juniors Football Team

They obviously take this business very seriously.

A Fatfield School class group

What is very interesting about this 1922 photograph is that the comedian Bobby Thompson (the 'little waster hissell') is in the centre of the back row. He was born in 4 The Staithes, Penshaw, the son of a deputy at North Biddick Colliery. He went to St Joseph's School, Washington at first. Then his parents died when he was just 8 years old. So he moved to live with a sister at Waggonway Terrace, Fatfield and then to live with another sister at New Penshaw in 1922. At school he was known as 'Little Tonka'. He wore glasses with only one lens in to correct a squint and tended to be the class comic to compensate for his vulnerability. He was described by a friend later as 'too funny to be taken seriously'. The fact that he was brought up by two sisters will have given him a lot of insight into the humour inherent in female conversation and gossip. He started to perform at Fatfield in a duo known as the 'guisers', wearing odd clothes and with blackened faces. Thompson specialised in the recitation of 'My Child You Have No Mother Now'. At the age of 14 he went to North Biddick Pit as a 'coupler-on lad' (ie. attaching the coal wagons – his brother Jimmy was a 'shuvver-in') for 7s 9d a week for eight hour shifts. This was supplemented by his dominoes income. Then in 1931 he gave up working in the pits and moved into show business in clubs and concert parties although he still had to supplement that by going into all sorts of jobs.

The Council Schools, Spout Lane Washington
There is snow on the road and roof.

The Glebe Schools, Washington
The Glebe Schools were built in the early years of the 20th Century. The Elementary School was built in 1908. It was joined by a Higher Grade School catering for secondary level in 1910. Later they became the John F. Kennedy Primary School.

A Glebe School classroom
This seems to be 1910. That makes it very early in the life of the school. There are not many photographs of classroom interiors. This is an excellent one of a girls class. There is a teacher to the left. One girl seems to have a magpie in her hair! The children are very attentive to the photographer. There is a nature study exhibition on the wall. There are 34 or 35 children. It is not clear what the significance of C175 is. It might be the photographer's record.

Glebe School children

This photograph was taken in the mid-1920s. The tall girl is a Nancy Goodwin. There are 44 children, boys and girls. Most of them look rather grim and suspicious. One or two have managed nice smiles though. The woman teacher looks very firm.

A Washington Infants School class group

This appears to be around 1900. It is certainly pre-First World War. There are 24 girls. Most of them are wearing white aprons. Some have very fine lace collars.

Iolanthe at Washington Secondary School
This was being performed in March, 1934. The school choir had a tested
repertoire which included Il Trovatore, The Gondoliers, The Pirates of
Penzance, The Mikado and Iolanthe. The choir was conducted by Mr T.G.
Wardle. The accompanist was Mr R.D.C. Wardle. The chorus of fairies was:
B. Chandler, R. Hunter, C. Russell, E. Smith, J. Hudspeth, M. Wilson,
J. Colquehoun, E. Smelt, J. Penaluna, B. Lennox, T.S. Waddle, E. Watson,
L. Thorpe, M. Dagg, L. Coxford, V. Watson, S. Plase, M. Lumsden, J.S. Waddle,
J. Sykes, R. Houlding, M. Elliott, M. Underwood, B. Davies and E. Le Roy.
A very attractive group of young ladies. This information is taken from a
handwritten and cyclostyled copy of a souvenir programme with photographic
prints stuck in.

Iolanthe at Washington Secondary School
Here are Phyllis (V. Duffey), the Earl of Mountararat
(L. Stewart) and the Earl Tolloller (J.W. Spencer).

Biddick School, Biddick Row, Washington
The date is 28th April 1905. The card was addressed to Mrs McKenzie, 16 Hedley Street, Wallsend. The message reads: 'Lizzie. Polly and I will leave here with the eleven train in the morning. Effie.' The building to the left is Biddick School which was opened in 1893. It became Columbia Primary School. It was closed in 1993.

A Biddick School class photograph

The Biddick School Washington Ceremony
This was in 1944. In the centre is Frederick Hill, a Washington historian and headmaster who was a leader of the movement to restore Washington Old Hall. The caption written by him for this was 'Typical annual ceremony at Biddick School, Washington, County Durham on the anniversary of George Washington's birthday on February 22, 1944!'. It is taken from his short book *Washington to White House* which was written for an American audience.

The Independence Day Annual Ceremony at Biddick School Probably in the 1940s. This is also taken from the book by Frederick Hill *Washington to White House* (1946). Sadly Mr Hill died in 1955 in the year of the opening of the restored Washington Old Hall.
He deserves to be well remembered by the people of Wearside not only as

teacher and local historian but also for taking a lead in that venture. He was awarded a medal by the United States Congress for his fostering of Anglo-American relations.

American Boy Scouts at Washington Old Hall

The date is 1965. The photograph is taken from the second edition of E. Underwood's *Washington Old Hall* (Boston 1959, 1967). He describes the event thus:

'In the Summer of 1965 the Second International Exchange of scouts came from New England and visited England and also Washington Hall as guests of Charles Sumner Bird, past president of the Old Colony Council Boy Scouts of America. The scouts were under the leadership of Murdo Dowds, District Commissioner and Willard K. Joyce of Weymouth. The Scout Executive of the Old Colony Council W.R. Speirs was also with the Troop as advisor and planner of the Exchange.

While the group was at Washington Old Hall the Rotary Club invited them to lunch. They showed the scouts the Hall grounds and the Town Hall of Washington. In the beautiful gardens of Washington Hall the visitors from the USA planted two cherry trees in memory of their visit, and as a salute from New England to the home of the Washington family in Old England.'

The Washington Greys

This photograph is also taken from E. Underwood's *Washington Old Hall*.

The Washington Greys Jazz Band was modelled on the famous Washington Greys of the New York State National Guard – the oldest military formation in the US armed forces. Their forerunners provided the bodyguard for General Washington

when he took office in New York on the 30th April, 1789.

A contingent of the Greys was present at the opening ceremony of the Old Hall in September 1955. They were dressed in 18th Century uniforms. It was decided to form a youth band which would wear copies of the Greys uniform and carry the Stars and Stripes. They were called the Washington District Band, the Washington Greys.

Washington Parish Church Bible Class
The 17 smart and attractive young women of the Washington Parish Church
Bible class. The scribbled message on this picture says that a Mrs Potts is third
from the right in the top row. The teacher looks very stern.

A Washington Street Party
There is a rather incongruous looking aspidistra in the right corner. There is a
nurse in a red cross tunic to the right as well. This appears to be a Victory
Street Party, but it could be a Coronation celebration.

Dame Margaret's Homes

There are actually two halls in Washington – the Old Hall and Washington Hall. The latter was built in 1854 for Sir Isaac Lowthian Bell. Bell was one of four industrialist son-in-laws of Hugh Pattinson. He was an ironmaster with blast furnaces near Washington Staithes. He was Lord Mayor of Newcastle in 1863 and was MP for several years. He and his son Sir Hugh Bell lived in the Hall until the 1870s. The builder was A.B. Higham of Newcastle. However it was considerably extended in 1865-7 by the famous architect Philip Webb.

The Hall stood empty from around 1878 to 1891. Sir Isaac then bequeathed it as a home for waifs and strays on condition that it be named after his beloved wife. Then in 1910 it became the Northern branch of Dr Barnardo's Homes. The children went to the Glebe Schools. Paradoxically it is also associated with the passing of legislation to control the use of climbing boys in chimneys. It was here that a seven year old child called Christopher Drummond was sent up and became trapped in the chimney. The sweep lit a fire to force the boy to struggle free but he died. This was one of the episodes used by Shaftesbury to support his reform.

Gertrude Bell was the daughter of Sir Hugh. She was born at the Hall in 1868. She became famous as scholar, poet, historian, mountain climber, explorer, linguist and diplomat. She could speak Arabic and other Eastern languages. She explored Syria and Arabia and established a range of friends and contacts there. In 1915 the British government used her to encourage the Arab leaders to support the Allies against Turkey. She played a part in the establishment of Iraq where she is still honoured. She died in 1926 in rather mysterious circumstances and is buried in Baghdad.

Dame Margaret's Homes
Whellan says of Dame Margaret's in its pre-Barnardo days:
'Dame Margaret's is partly a home for waifs and strays, but its chief objective is to provide a convalescent home for children from hospitals. It is dependent on voluntary subscription, and caters for about 100 children. Girls are trained as domestic servants, and boys are apprenticed out to various trades at the proper age.' This scene is possibly from around 1910.

Children playing in Brady Square
In the first edition of this book we captioned this photograph as an Usworth playground. We received many letters pointing out our error and we thank all those who helped us.

The opening of the Washington Station Boys Club
This is the opening of the Washington Station Boys Club in Glebe Crescent in July 1936 by Prince Henry, the Duke of Gloucester. Confusingly there were two huts in the same grounds. The Geoffrey Newall Scout and Guide Hut was funded by Mr Newall. It was in use until 1966 and then replaced by a brick structure. The hut opened by the Duke was for more general use by youth groups. There are several boys on the left who are not in any sort of uniform. The hut was opened officially by Prince Henry. Various dignitaries were presented to him and:

'The Duke expressed pleasure at two boys playing chess. He asked them if they liked it and was told that they had learned it at school.'

During the visit it was announced that the club was to be adopted by the staff of the Ministry of Agriculture and Fisheries and that the staff would assist the club financially. It was situated at the south end of Glebe Crescent on the east side of the street.

The Geoffrey Newall Scout and Guide Hut

Washington Library Pictures

p1, 11T, 15B, 20T, 24T, 26B, 32T, 38B, 52B, 55T, 56B, 58T, 60T, 66B, 67T, 67B, 70T, 70B, 71T, 72T, 72B, 73T, 73B, 74B, 76T, 76B, 83T, 85T, 88T, 89T, 90B, 91T, 91B, 92T, 93B, 104B, 105T, 105B, 108B, 109B, 110B, 116T, 117B, 120B, 126

Many thanks to Ian S. Carr for his photograph of Washington Station on page 92.

SOURCES AND FURTHER READING

There is very little available on Washington. The sources listed below are held at the Washington or Sunderland Central Library but some of them are not available for borrowing. The most recent and most useful coverage is:

Sutherland, A. and Wood, J. *Washington Then and Now* (Wear Books,1993).

You would do well to consult a useful undergraduate dissertation on the area in general:

Brookes, S. *The Development of Washington in the Nineteenth Century* (Sunderland Polytechnic unpublished dissertation, 1982)

There are some useful antiquarian works:
Bennett, C. *Washington Local History* (1967)
Hill, Frederick *Local Records of Washington No. 3, Local Stories of Fact, Fiction and Folklore* (Andrew Reid and Co. Ltd., 1944)
Hill, Frederick *Local Records of Washington No. 1, History of Washington Parish Church* (Northumberland Press Ltd., 1929)
Hill, Frederick *The Pitman of Biddick and the Earldom of Perth* (private, no date)
Hind, Albert *History and Folklore of Old Washington* (private, 1976)
Hind, Albert *History of Fatfield and Harraton* (private, 1974)
Hind, Albert *Penshaw Monument* (private, 1978)

There are some useful collections of newscuttings in the reserve stock of Washington Library:

Newscuttings 1900-1950
(These seem to have been kept by a Newalls employee)
Smith, C.A. *History of Washington* from the *Sunderland Echo* (1963). Newspaper cuttings.
Smith, C. A. *The Lambton Family* - Articles from the *Sunderland Echo* (1962)

On the Washington New Town there are two 'official' histories. These are one-sided of course, but quite thorough for all that.

Holley, S. *Washington: Quicker by Quango. The History of Washington New Town 1964-1983* (Publications for Companies, 1983)
McLelland, G. *Washington: Over and Out. The Story of Washington New Town 1983-1988* (Publications for Companies, 1988)

Then there are a number of other works which you may find useful:

Colls, Robert *The Pitmen of the Northern Coalfield* (Manchester University Press, 1987)
Goodman, S. *Gertrude Bell* (1985)
Hoole, K. *Regional History of the Railways of Great Britain Vol. 4 The North East* (David and Charles, 1974
Joseph Cook Sons & Co. Ltd. *Colliery and Mining Engineers Illustrated Catalogue*. Cooks supplied not only the wagons and smaller implements but entire pit head gear systems and prefabricated structures. This catalogue gives a good idea as to the scale of the business.
Johnson, M. *Washington Church: A history and guide* (1984)
Lewis, M.J.T. *Early Wooden Railways* (Routledge and Kegan Paul, 1970). Only a few sections are relevant to this area but it helps to set the context of the early mining and coal export industries.
Morris, John (ed.) *Boldon Book: Northumberland and Durham* (Phillimore, 1982)
Nicholson, Dave *Bobby Thompson: A Private Audience* (1994). Thompson's recollections of life in the Fatfield-Penshaw area are especially illuminating. The problem with him was that he was such a comedian off-stage as well that he was difficult to interview sensibly.
Patterson, W.M. *Northern Primitive Methodism* (E. Dalton, 1909)
Purdon, G. *Cotia Pit: Local Reflections and the Story of Harraton* (private, no date)
Shelley, B. *The Little Waster* (Inkerman Publications Ltd, 1979) Interesting recollections, albeit brief, by Thompson.
Turner and Newall Ltd. *The First Fifty Years: 1920-70* (1970)
Illustrations and Drawings of Some of the Leading Manufactures of Joseph Cook and Son Engineers, Washington Ironworks, Co. Durham (1898)
Whellan, F. and Co. *History, Topography and Directory of the County Palatine of Durham* (2nd Edition, 1894)

On the subject of postcards you might find the following useful:

Alderson, Frederick *The Comic Postcard in English Life* (David and Charles, 1970)
Byatt, Anthony *Picture Postcards and their Publishers* (Golden Age Postcard Books, 1978)
Carline, Richard *Pictures in the Post* (Gordon Fraser, 1971)
Hill, C.W. *Discovering Picture Postcards* (Shire, 1970)
Holt,Tonie and Holt, Valmai *Picture Postcards of the Golden Age* (MacGibbon and Kee, 1971)
Staff, Frank *The Picture Postcard and its Origins* (Lutterworth Press, 1966)

Magazines:

Picture Postcard Monthly
The British Postcard Collectors' Magazine